W9-AGZ-709

This book was donated to the
TULARE COUNTY LIBRARY
through a grant from

BLUE CROSS of CALIFORNIA
and the
FRIENDS OF THE
TULARE COUNTY LIBRARY

J 616.8526 GAY
Gay, Kathlyn.
Eating disorders
  :anorexia, bulimia, an
VISA
    1 9 MAR 2004

—Diseases and People—

EATING DISORDERS—
Anorexia, Bulimia, and Binge Eating

Kathlyn Gay

Enslow Publishers, Inc.

40 Industrial Road   PO Box 38
Box 398   Aldershot
Berkeley Heights, NJ 07922 Hants GU12 6BP
USA   UK

http://www.enslow.com

TULARE COUNTY LIBRARY

Copyright © 2003 by Kathlyn Gay

All rights reserved.

No part of this book may be reproduced by any means
without the written permission of the publisher.

Library of Congress Cataloging-in-Publication Data

Gay, Kathlyn.
    Eating disorders / Kathlyn Gay.
        p. cm.
    Includes bibliographical references and index.
    ISBN 0-7660-1894-6
    1. Eating disorders—Juvenile literature. [1. Eating disorders.]
    I.Title.
    RC552.E18 G39 2003
    616.85'26—dc21   2001006769

Printed in the United States of America

10 9 8 7 6 5 4 3 2 1

To Our Readers:
We have done our best to make sure all Internet Addresses in this book were active and
appropriate when we went to press. However, the author and the publisher have no control
over and assume no liability for the material available on those Internet sites or on other Web
sites they may link to. Any comments or suggestions can be sent by e-mail to
comments@enslow.com or to the address on the back cover.

Every effort has been made to locate all copyright holders of material used in this book. If any
errors or omissions have occurred, corrections will be made in future editions of this book.

Illustration Credits: Associated Press/Twentieth Century Fox, p. 27; © Corel
Corporation, pp. 15, 31; © Díamar Interactive Corp., pp. 11, 43; © Robin Lasser
and Kathryn Sylva, p. 80; © Starlane Photo, p. 34; Eckehard Schulz/Associated
Press, p. 51; Enslow Publishers, Inc., p. 23, 93; From Psychological Medicine, 1982,
p. 67; Jimi Celeste/Fashion Wire Daily, p. 18; Kathlyn Gay, pp. 36, 42, 57, 77, 84;
Oscar Burriel/Science Photo Library, p. 48; Photo courtesy of The Renfrew Center,
p. 70; Reprinted with permission from the National Osteoporosis Foundation,
Washington, DC 20036, p. 40; Sheila Terry/Science Photo Library, p. 63.

Cover Illustration: Oscar Burriel/Science Photo Library

Contents

EATING DISORDERS

What are eating disorders? In general, eating disorders (EDs) are characterized by extremely abnormal eating behaviors. Two types of EDs are anorexia nervosa and bulimia nervosa, more commonly known as anorexia and bulimia. Victims of anorexia have an intense fear of gaining weight and starve themselves, while bulimics eat, but purge themselves of food by forced vomiting or by the excess use of laxatives. Binge eating has been also recognized recently as an eating disorder. Sometimes called compulsive overeating, binge eating is similar to bulimia except that binge eaters do not purge themselves of excess food.

Who are the victims of eating disorders? Although EDs were once thought to affect primarily wealthy white women, people of all racial, ethnic, and economic backgrounds suffer from the diseases. Most sufferers are girls and young women, but boys and men are increasingly becoming affected by these disorders. An estimated eight to ten million Americans seek treatment for EDs. Out of that number, about one million are males. Most of the sufferers are products of Western, particularly American, culture, which prizes thinness in women and lean, muscular bodies in men.

What are the symptoms? Both anorexics and bulimics place an abnormal emphasis on weight and body image and are usually secretive about their rituals, although bulimics may be less inclined than anorexics to hide their illness. People with eating disorders do not like to eat in public; fanatically count calories; experience dramatic weight changes; exhibit low self esteem; withdraw socially; and may exercise excessively—that is, for many hours—in unsupervised running, weight-lifting, calisthenics, or other activities designed to "burn off" calories.

How are the disorders treated? The most common treatment is a combination of psychotherapy, medication, and nutrition counseling. In some cases, especially in anorexics who develop medical complications such as anemia and irregular heart rhythms, hospitalization may be necessary before treatment can begin.

How are the disorders prevented? Education is one of the primary measures used to prevent eating disorders. This is often accomplished through organizations and individuals dedicated to alerting the public about symptoms of eating disorders and their risk factors.

1

The Enemy is Food

When Terri, a Florida resident, was in high school, she began a liquid diet to lose weight. Three years after she graduated and was married, she was still dieting, hoping to trim her figure so she would look good in a bikini at the beach. Some of Terri's friends and relatives believe that this was the beginning of an eating disorder—either anorexia or bulimia or both. No one can be certain because Terri suffered a heart attack in 1990 and has been in a coma ever since. She cannot breathe on her own and is given food supplements and liquid through a feeding tube.

Over the years, Terri's condition has created great controversy and resulted in lawsuits. Her husband is convinced that she will not recover and believes that she would want her feeding tube removed, allowing her to die. Her parents believe that even though Terri cannot speak, she can react to them and they are fighting to keep Terri alive.

Doctors say that Terri's heart attack was brought on by low levels of potassium, one of the chemicals the body needs to make muscles work—especially the heart muscle. This is just one sign of a possible eating disorder. Other signals include the fact that Terri had abdominal pains before her heart attack, which often occurs when a person refuses to eat or frequently vomits to get rid of food. In addition, Terri had irregular menstrual periods, another common symptom of anorexia or bulimia in females.[1]

Terri's heart attack and tragic result have underscored a fact that many people are beginning to heed: Women with eating disorders are twelve times more likely to die of heart attacks than women who eat normally.

Distorted Views

In spite of health risks, many people—both female and male—develop eating disorders because they have distorted views of their body weight and shape. They often say they are too fat, even though they are of normal weight, and they hate looking at themselves in the mirror. They believe that if they have "perfect" bodies, they will feel better about themselves.

Many sufferers have low self esteem and are in poor physical health, as was reflected in the film, *Dying to be Thin*, shown in December 2000 on NOVA, a public broadcasting service program. A companion presentation was posted on NOVA Online. Producers of the site asked viewers who had suffered or were currently suffering from eating disorders to share their experiences so they could help others. As a result, dozens of stories were posted on the NOVA Web site through the month of December. A constant theme came through in the writings:

"No matter how hard I tried, I couldn't get thin, and it was the central problem of my very young life."—Anonymous

"Thin to me = success, a picture of perfection, a package that needs to be complete, beautiful, perfect to present to the outside world."—Anonymous

"Cheerleaders were all the rage in high school, and I was determined to become one. But they were all thin, pretty, and sooo confident. I spent most of my time fantasizing a life where I was special and that meant being thin."—Karen

"There is not one minute of the day that I cannot think about losing weight."—Trisha

"I want to get . . . thinner, prettier, more perfect. The only thing that scares me is, I know I am dying."—Anne

"The sick thing about anorexia is that when people say 'You're way too thin, you look horrible. . . . ' that's about the best compliment you feel you can receive. And all this negativity...only made my obsession stronger and gave me a sense of accomplishment." —Anonymous[2]

Most of the writers posting on this Web site were in their early teenage years when their eating disorders began, although some described problems when they were as young as five or six years old. Many struggled for years to overcome anorexia or bulimia or both. Some succeeded and are recovering, while others continue their harmful practices because, as one girl wrote: "The thought of death seems much better than…being fat, which my reason or logic tells me is absurd. But there is no logic in this disorder. When it rules, it's the only thing that matters."[3]

Anyone with an eating disorder considers food an enemy and something she or he has to control. In fact, the belief that one needs to be in control is as much a part of the disease as abnormal eating behaviors.

Some Statistics

Eating disorders are common in most industrialized countries, including European nations, Australia, Canada, Japan, New Zealand, South Africa, and the United States.[4] How many people in the United States suffer from EDs? There are no firm statistics, because people with these disorders tend to hide or deny they are engaged in unhealthy behavior.

Denial is even more pronounced for males than for females, according to psychiatrist Thomas Holbrook, who himself has recovered from anorexia and is now director of the Eating Disorder Center at Rogers Memorial Hospital in Oconomowoc, Wisconsin, located between Milwaukee and Madison. In Holbrook's view, it is difficult for men and boys to acknowledge that they "care so much about how their bodies look."[5]

In addition, doctors do not always recognize symptoms, which may be mistaken for health problems ranging from those linked to fad diets to drug abuse. When doctors do diagnose full-fledged eating disorders, they are not required to

Although boys may exercise and participate in sports to get into shape, it is sometimes hard for them to acknowledge that they care how their bodies look.

report these diseases to a health agency. But according to estimates by various ED organizations and health centers, about one out of every one hundred adolescent females develop anorexia. An estimated two to five of every one hundred women suffer from bulimia, a disorder that is ten times more common in females than in males. Without treatment between 10 and 20 percent of those diagnosed with anorexia will eventually die due to complications of the disease. Yet between 60 and 80 percent of people with eating disorders respond successfully to treatment.[6]

Diabetes and Eating Disorders

Clearly, an eating disorder is a dangerous disease, but when it is combined with diabetes, the health consequences can be deadly. The American Diabetes Association defines diabetes as "a disease in which the body does not produce or properly use insulin, a hormone that is needed to convert sugar, starches and other food into energy needed for daily life." To stay alive, thousands of diabetics must take daily insulin shots, which help reduce blood sugar. In addition, diabetics must control their weight and the types of food they eat in order to maintain good health.

No one is sure how many diabetics have eating disorders. However, health-care practitioners say that the combination is common, especially among young people. Why? Because a diabetic's focus on food and weight can set the stage for developing an eating disorder. In fact, a diabetic may become preoccupied with food or think of food as dangerous, something to avoid, thus leading to anorexia or bulimia.

Rebellion is another factor that could lead a diabetic to develop an eating disorder. Parents or other family members are apt to be overly protective of young diabetics, constantly monitoring what and how much they eat. Diabetics may resent such supervision and try to take control over their food and weight.

Some diabetics with eating disorders try to take control by reducing their insulin dosage, an extremely dangerous practice. These diabetics reason that because insulin can cause weight gain, they can stay thin with smaller doses. But less insulin causes blood sugar to rise. If blood sugar is not maintained in a healthy manner, a diabetic is at great risk for damage to the eyes, nerves, and kidneys. In fact, every system of the body is in jeopardy.

One woman, Miriam Tucker, who was diagnosed with diabetes when she was nine years old, explained that as a teenager she ate whatever she liked, deliberately running her blood sugar high so she would not gain weight. She explained that she:

> would do things like wait till my mom left the room, then eat everything in sight. Then I'd lie and say I didn't eat a thing.
> . . . every day I would decide to be "good," to eat nothing but vegetables and maybe an apple. And when I slipped— which I did almost every day—I felt terrible, worthless, "bad."[7]

As an adult, Tucker began to have problems with her sight and her kidneys. She eventually realized she had to follow her doctor's advise by eating a balanced diet, testing her blood sugar regularly, and taking the appropriate amount of insulin.

Eating Disorders Among Celebrities

Over the past twenty to thirty years, educational programs in the United States and other countries have attempted to focus public attention on eating disorders. These efforts have been reinforced by entertainers, models, and sports celebrities, who have revealed their struggles with abnormal eating behaviors.

One of the most famous people who reportedly suffered from an eating disorder was Diana, Princess of Wales. Several of her biographers contend that during the 1980s, Diana would binge and then purge on occasion, a practice that she once jokingly called a new way to diet. But the binge-and-purge episodes became more frequent, and she soon fit the criteria for an eating disorder. After years of denying she had a problem, she sought treatment and therapy with a London psychiatrist. Diana's recovery process appeared to be successful, although it is uncertain whether she ever completely overcame her eating disorder before her tragic death in a 1997 car accident.

Years before Diana's struggles were reported, the death of a famous entertainer of the 1980s, Karen Ann Carpenter, brought public attention to the terrible health consequences of eating disorders. Carpenter died of heart failure caused by her long-term dieting and misuse of medications to lose weight. About two years before her death she had started to recover from anorexia, but her repeated misuse of laxatives and other

It has been reported by several news agencies that Princess Diana of Wales suffered from an eating disorder.

medications permanently damaged her heart. While anorexic, she had routinely taken between seventy and eighty laxative pills at a time to produce bowel movements. She also took syrup of ipecac, a medication used to induce vomiting in cases of accidental poisoning. In addition, according to her therapist, Carpenter took large doses of a thyroid medication to speed up her metabolism—increase her energy.[8]

Since Carpenter's death, other celebrities have gone public with their stories in attempts to prevent such tragedies. One who has made an impact is famous gymnast Cathy Rigby, who suffered from both anorexia and bulimia. She overcame her problems and went on to become a highly successful entertainer, gaining stardom in *Peter Pan*—the Broadway musical and the film, both produced during the 1990s.

Rigby and her husband Tom McCoy own a successful production company, and together they have created a "VidBook," a multimedia learning environment posted on the Web. As Rigby notes in her opening statement introducing the site, "For twelve years, I was bulimic. I know the headaches and the heartaches that accompany this disorder."

When she was a young child, Rigby was "shy, introverted and insecure," and tried to prove herself through sports. Gymnastics became "the perfect escape for a ten-year-old with growing image problems" because she was praised and felt worthwhile. But she admits, "When my weight increased, as it naturally does during puberty, I was terrified. . . . I made a decision never to gain weight again. This was the beginning of my own bulimic behavior."[9] Today, one of Rigby's goals is to help people with eating disorders overcome their problems.

Other famous gymnasts, such as Kathy Johnson, Nadia Comaneci, and Christy Henrich, also struggled with EDs. In 1988, a United States judge at a gymnastic meet in Hungary told Henrich that she needed to lose weight if she wanted to make the Olympic team. Her weight-reduction efforts eventually led to anorexia and bulimia. At one time, she weighed only forty-seven pounds. Because of her self-starvation, she experienced multiple organ failure in 1994 and died at the age of twenty-two.

Waiflike models are another group often afflicted with eating disorders. Fashion model Magali Amedei, who has been on the covers of such magazines as *Vogue, Elle, Cosmopolitan, Marie Claire, Harpers & Queen, Glamour,* and *Harper's Bazaar,* can attest to that. She is one of the first top models to publicly admit having an eating disorder, and since 1998, she has spoken out about her seven-year battle with and victory over bulimia. She took part in a one-month tour in 1999, speaking in schools and colleges across the United States as part of the outreach program of the American Anorexia Bulimia Association (AABA). In a press release regarding her tour, she expressed hope that:

> by telling my personal story, others who are suffering will
> see that their shame is unwarranted and their disease is
> treatable and curable. I am living proof of that. . . . Eating
> disorders are diseases with the same addictive behavior of
> alcoholism. . . . I consider this tour an important part of

Model Kate Dillon, who once suffered from anorexia, has set out to raise awareness of eating disorders.

my recovery, and if I only help one person by speaking out, then I will know that I have made a difference.[10]

Another model who has set out to make a difference is Kate Dillon. She was once anorexic, but is now her normal weight and lectures on body image and self-esteem. Dillon appeared in the TV film *Dying to be Thin* and its counterpart Web site, where she explained that she stopped being a part of the thinness fashion because it "inflicts these ridiculous ideals upon our culture." However, she is still a successful model, promoting the concept that beauty can be measured in diverse ways. She says that, at the age of twenty:

> I made a decision to be true to myself no matter what. I wanted to be someone I admired, not the person I thought I *should* be. So, I committed myself to a journey I'm still on, a journey in which I embrace every ounce of who I am, the good parts and the less groovy parts! I enjoy life.[11]

2

The History of Anorexia and Bulimia

For the past two decades, personal stories, news reports, books, Web sites, TV shows, and magazine articles on anorexia and bulimia have steadily increased in number. But eating disorders are not newly discovered problems. Eating behaviors similar to those of today's ED sufferers were described in the writings of ancient Egypt, Persia, and China.

According to some medical historians, in 1694, Dr. Richard Morton published the first case history of what appeared to be symptoms of anorexia in his *Phthisiologia: or a Treatise of Consumptions*. But social historian Joan Jacob Brumberg argues that the case Morton described "included some of the symptoms of anorexia nervosa; but he saw other symptoms that are not part of the modern diagnosis." Brumberg contends that today's understanding of the disorder tends to influence what the "historical evidence" will be.[1]

During the 1870s, Sir William Gull gave anorexia its name—which means "nervous loss of appetite." However, loss of appetite is associated with many illnesses, and anorexics usually do not lose their appetites until they are dangerously ill. The more meaningful definition used today is "severe disturbances in eating behavior."[2]

Symptoms of bulimia, from a Greek word meaning great or oxlike hunger, were also apparent centuries ago. "Ancient Romans overindulged at lavish banquets and then relieved themselves in a vomitorium (lavatory chamber that accommodated vomiting) so they could return to the feast and continue eating," states the organization Anorexia Nervosa and Related Eating Disorders, Inc.[3] Whether this practice was actually bulimia is not clear, because bulimia was not recognized as a specific illness until the twentieth century. However, over the years, there have been numerous descriptions of people who were intensely fixated on food, overate, and then vomited. In 1980, bulimia nervosa was described as a symptom of an eating disorder in the third edition of the American Psychiatric Association's standard reference guide, *Diagnostic and Statistical Manual, Third Edition* (DSM-III). The manual contains internationally accepted terms and diagnoses used in psychiatric practice. When a revised edition (DSM-III-R) was issued in 1985, bulimia nervosa was officially listed as a disease.

From "Holy" Starvation to Modern-Day EDs

During the Middle Ages, between the twelfth and sixteenth centuries, extremely devout women known in the Christian church as saints refused to eat and took part in prolonged fasts as a way to show devotion to God. Although male saints also have fasted or restricted their diets for religious purposes, they were few in number. "In the medieval period fasting was fundamental to the model of female holiness," according to author Joan Jacobs Brumberg. She wrote:

> The medieval woman's capacity for survival without eating meant that she found other forms of food: prayer provided sustenance, as did the Christian eucharist—the body and blood of Christ—injested as wafer and wine. Women who were reputed to have lived without food—that is, without eating anything except the eucharist—were particularly numerous in the thirteenth through fifteenth centuries.[4]

Over the centuries, fasting to show devotion has been a traditional practice in varied religions and has been a part of political movements. But Rudolph M. Bell contends in his book, *Holy Anorexia*, that medieval female Christian saints hated their bodies because they considered them corrupt, which they believed prevented their own salvation as well as that of their loved ones. Because the flesh could not be tamed, it had to be destroyed. Their religious devotion and need for salvation and perfection sometimes led the women to starve themselves to death.

Saint Catherine of Siena died at the age of thirty-three from her unhealthy eating practices.

Catherine Benincasa, known as Catherine of Siena (1347–1380), was one of the saints who constantly struggled for perfection. She wanted to be a martyr for Christ. At the age of seventeen, she became a lay member of a Dominican order of widows who cared for the sick and poor.

Catherine apparently had demonic visions and temptations, so to counteract them and achieve greater "holiness," she existed on a diet of bread, water, and raw vegetables. At times, she ate twigs so that she could purge herself by vomiting. Her behavior eventually led to her death at the age of thirty-three.

In an epilogue to Bell's *Holy Anorexia*, William N. Davis wrote that "holy anorexia and anorexia nervosa represent remarkably similar conditions," although "one is driven by the desire to be holy and the other by the desire to be thin. The point is that anorexics in the fourteenth century and those [today] do not want to eat because they abhor the consequences. And whether in the service of holiness or thinness, they determinedly relish the effects of starvation."[5]

Jennifer Egan, in an article for the *New York Times Magazine*, explained that the behavior of some fourteenth century saints:

> foreshadowed that of a great many women today for whom power and suffering—often self-inflicted—are curiously intertwined. Modern-day anorexics, bulimics, and self-injurers experience an illusion of control through disciplining or mutilating their bodies, echoing the pious self-punishments of Catherine's time. The lives of

Catherine and other saints like her can help to explain why these impulses persist among women—from athletes and models to Diana, Princess of Wales.[6]

The "illusion of control" that Egan described is often apparent in comments from ED sufferers. Many say they have strict parents and the only way they can feel in control is when they choose not to eat or to purge themselves of food. Anorexics often express pride in having the will power to resist food; they describe feelings of guilt if they "give in" and eat something tempting like a chocolate chip cookie. In some cases, they taste or chew food, but spit it out before it travels to the stomach.

Some seek attention and love from parents or others, and when that is not forthcoming, controlling hunger and food is a way of controlling the need for love. Anorexia is a coping skill, some say, and sufferers starve themselves into numbness so they won't have to face change or feel the effects of disappointing relationships.

The struggle for perfection is also common. People with eating disorders try to achieve nearly impossible goals. In school they try to get perfect grades, seek perfect relationships, and attempt to develop perfect bodies. Many gain a sense of power when they can maintain control over their bodies, particularly those who participate in sports like gymnastics, swimming, wrestling, long-distance running, or in demanding professions such as ballet, figure skating, acting, and fashion modeling.

Following Fashion

For centuries women have followed any number of fashion trends to be "with it" and appear attractive. In the late 1800s, for example, actress Lillian Russell was considered an ideal beauty, with an ample figure weighing in at about two hundred pounds. Women wore bustles to accentuate or amplify their behinds. They tied themselves into rib-breaking corsets to pinch in their waists and push out their bosoms.

Fashion also has dictated that women appear thin and flat-chested, as was the case between the 1920s and 1930s. Then, in the 1950s, the woman who represented the ideal female body was Marilyn Monroe, with her hourglass figure. During that same decade, the Barbie doll, manufactured by Mattel, appeared. Early in the 1960s, her companions, including her boyfriend Ken, came on the scene. Later in the decade, male action figures like G. I. Joe, created by Hasbro, became popular.

Such toys have been controversial ever since their inception. Barbie dolls have been tall, thin, and buxom, while male figures have been lean and muscular. Over the years, though, their proportions have changed, with Barbie becoming more buxom and male figures sporting torsos with more wedge-like shapes. Their dimensions would be impossible for real people to achieve. For example, to obtain the muscular proportions of a G. I. Joe, Luke Skywalker, Ironman, or other muscular action figure, a five-foot, ten-inch man would have to have a chest measuring sixty-two inches and biceps measuring thirty-two inches.[7] This unrealistic model influences many young boys.

Marilyn Monroe, with her hourglass figure, represented the ideal female body in the 1950s.

In an article for *Time* magazine, Amy Dickinson noted that along with increasing rates of anorexia and bulimia among boys, they:

> are falling victim to a newly named disorder: muscle dysmorphia (also called bigorexia)—the conviction that one is too small. This syndrome is marked by an obsession with the size and shape of your body, constant working out and weight lifting (even if you aren't involved in sports) and the use of supplements to 'bulk up.'[8]

Helping to sustain the ideal of thin body types for young girls was British fashion model Twiggy. She arrived in the United States in 1967, standing five feet, seven inches tall and weighing ninety-one pounds. Her almost instant popularity triggered a shift in average sizes and weights for fashion models.

During the 1970s and 1980s, thinness gave way to the toned look, and advertisers promoted fitness with exercise equipment and tapes and various diets. That trend continued into the 1990s. But at the same time authors like Susan Faludi (*Backlash: The Undeclared War Against American Women*, 1991) and Naomi Wolf (*The Beauty Myth*, 1991) warned girls and women that they were being manipulated to buy products that the fashion, diet, and cosmetic industries dictated were needed in order to be beautiful, popular, and acceptable among boys and men.

Other writers during the mid-1990s began to sound alarms about media images described as "heroin chic." The term was applied to male and female models who looked gaunt, pale, glassy-eyed, and anorexic. In short, the models appeared to be close to death. The images, especially those advertising Calvin Klein clothing, drew many protests from anti-drug groups. After the death of fashion photographer Davide Sorrenti from a heroin overdose in 1997, then President Bill Clinton addressed the U.S. Conference of Mayors to point out that fashion leaders admitted the images "made heroin addiction seem glamorous and sexy and cool." But the president warned that heroin can kill, and emphasized that glamorizing addiction is not needed to sell clothes.[9]

The president's speech and public protests prompted the fashion industry to change its approach, and now wholesome and healthy images are supposed to be in style. But most models still maintain skeleton-like bodies. The messages they portray in advertisements for countless products are clear: thin equates with health and happiness. These images are admired and idolized by millions of young people who want to look just like the models—even if it means becoming anorexic or bulimic.

Yet, "picture-perfect models are less than perfect," as nutritionist Debra Waterhouse pointed out in her book, *Like Mother, Like Daughter: How Women Are Influenced by Their Mothers' Relationship with Food—and How to Break the Pattern.* "Expert makeup artists provide the perfect coloring, hairstylists add body and shine, and skilled photographers take hundreds of photographs with perfect lighting, angles, and shadows. Then, after the best photo is chosen, up to four hours of retouching begins to eliminate any evidence of pores, lines, or imperfections. At times, the head of one model may be used on the body of another."[10]

The point Waterhouse and many other writers make is that attempting to develop a body shape and size based on a fashion ideal is like chasing after an illusion. To put it bluntly: it is phony.

Nevertheless, trying to conform to the skinny version of beauty preoccupies a majority of American girls. A study reported in 1999 in the medical journal *Pediatrics* showed that fashion magazine images had a strong impact on girls from the fifth through twelfth grade. Of the 548 students in the study, 69 percent reported that magazine images influenced their idea of the perfect body shape, and 47 percent reported wanting to lose weight because of the images.[11]

Negative Self-Images

Among children aged eight to ten, about half the girls and one third of the boys are dissatisfied with their size, according to the Harvard Eating Disorders Center. Girls want to be thinner (like models or actresses) and boys want to be heavier and more muscular (like body-builders).[12] Frequently, such dissatisfaction can lead to disordered eating, anorexia, or bulimia.

Body dissatisfaction even affects girls as young as five years old, according to a survey published in *Pediatrics* in 2001. Girls have negative self-images when their weight is above average, say researchers, who are conducting a long-term study of 197 girls in a Northeastern community, which has not been

An increasing number of men with eating disorders can be found working out for hours to become more lean and muscular.

identified to protect the children's identities. The study also revealed that girls whose parents were concerned about their weight were more likely to see themselves as inferior. "It was startling," one of the specialists conducting the study told a reporter. "If girls are showing these issues at age five, it doesn't look hopeful for what is going to happen to them as teenagers or young women."[13] In short, the low levels of self-concept could set the stage for eating disorders in the girls' later years.

Eating disorders also affect immigrants to the United States. Counselors at ED centers in the Washington, D.C., area say that the number of immigrant girls and young women seeking treatment has been steadily increasing. A similar situation exists in New York City and Los Angeles. Eating disorders seem prevalent especially among teenagers whose parents immigrated from Latin America, Africa, the Middle East, or Asia. As the *Washington Post* reported, "Immigrant women and girls often feel a distinct kind of pressure to conform to American beauty standards because they look different from the majority of the population."[14]

3

Detecting Anorexia

In the early 1990s, TV star Tracey Gold, who played Carol on the TV show *Growing Pains*, met Roby Marshall, a production assistant for the show. They soon began dating. After a few dates, Marshall said he knew that Tracey was hiding something, because they would plan events, "always around a meal—let's go for lunch, let's go for dinner. But I'd be the one that's eating and Tracey is having a diet coke."[1]

In 1992, Gold became "so thin, you could see her veins pulsing, see her veins through her skin," Roby said. He and most of the cast thought she was going to die. Tracey was removed from the show and admitted to the hospital. After hospitalization, she spent a year visiting a doctor every day and working on her recovery from anorexia, which actually had begun long before, when she was just twelve years old. She credits her recovery on her primary motivation: to get married.

Actress Tracey Gold suffered from anorexia since the age of twelve, but after her hospitalization in 1992, she has made a wonderful recovery.

Roby, who is devoted to Tracey, said that they could not get married until she could have a bite of the wedding cake. "That may seem silly," Tracey said, "but the truth is there was a time [when] no way could I have a bite of wedding cake."

Following Tracey's recovery, the couple married in 1994. Her career has flourished with appearances in numerous TV movies. She frequently discusses her anorexia and has been an inspiration to others with the disorder. She said the positive reactions she gets from talking about anorexia "is worth everything I've been through."[2]

Singing star Anne Murray of Canada said she knew in 1997 that "something was very wrong" with her daughter, Dawn Langstroth, who was then sixteen years old. Murray told reporters that she realized there were recognizable signs. "But it didn't click because I didn't want it to."[3] Dawn seldom ate, exercised obsessively, worried about whether she was thin enough to become a model, and read numerous magazine articles about eating disorders. "Looking back, I wonder how I missed it, it was so obvious," Murray said.[4]

Dawn eventually admitted that she was ill and forced her mother to see the truth. After learning about Dawn's symptoms—she felt listless and depressed and exercised compulsively—Murray immediately took her daughter to a specialist, who diagnosed anorexia. Dawn then went to a treatment center in Florida and has recovered. Now she and her mother tell their story, hoping their experiences will help other anorexic victims.

Disordered Eating

As people become more aware of EDs, they also recognize signs of the diseases. Signals may first appear as some type of disordered eating.

Disordered eating is a fairly recent term with varied definitions. Generally, though, it includes such behavior as skipping meals, restricting certain foods, expressing guilt about eating some foods, feeling fat even though thin, not eating one day and then overeating the next, purging by vomiting or using laxatives, and exercising for hours to "burn off" fat.

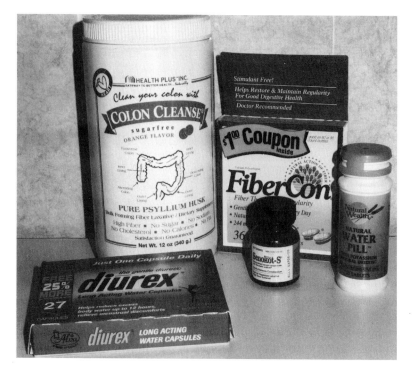

Laxatives and diuretics (water pills) are commonly used by bulimics.

Millions of girls and women and an increasing number of boys and men have some of these disordered or unhealthy eating habits. However, they may not develop bona fide eating disorders, which are psychiatric illnesses that fit the criteria spelled out in the *Diagnostic and Statistical Manual of Mental Disorders* published by the American Psychiatric Association.

Although most preadolescents and adolescents do not develop eating disorders, young people in these age groups are at risk, particularly if they have low self-esteem, are dependent on others for approval, and have difficulty socializing and becoming independent. Many young people also are influenced by social pressures to be attractive, which they usually interpret as the need to be thin. When a young person's desire to be thin leads to excessive dieting, she or he may be at great risk for the onset of an eating disorder.[5]

According to the National Association of Anorexia Nervosa and Associated Eating Disorders (ANAD), 10 percent of those diagnosed with EDs reported onset of their illness at ten years of age or younger; 33 percent between the ages of eleven and fifteen; and 43 percent between the ages of sixteen and twenty.[6]

Diagnosing Anorexia

Unlike disordered eating, the criteria for eating disorders are specific. They are described in the fourth edition of *Diagnostic and Statistical Manual of Mental Disorders* (DSM-IV). The manual states that the essential symptoms of anorexia nervosa are characterized by:

- Refusal to maintain a normal level of body weight for age and size.
- Intense fear of gaining weight or becoming fat, even though underweight.
- Disturbance in the way in which one's body weight or shape is experienced or perceived.
- Delay in the onset of menses for preadolescent girls, or for those who have started menstruating, no periods for at least three consecutive cycles.

There are also subtypes of anorexia nervosa. The first is the restricting type, in which "the person has not regularly engaged in binge-eating or purging behavior" but loses weight primarily through dieting, fasting, or excessive exercise.[7]

Binge-eating/purging is the second type. Those in this category binge eat and purge through self-induced vomiting or the misuse of laxatives and enemas, medications that increase bowel movements, and diuretics (water pills) that increase urination. Some "do not binge eat, but do regularly purge after the consumption of small amounts of food."[8]

Health Consequences of Anorexia

Eating disorders can cause severe health problems, and anyone with full-blown anorexia is at risk for serious illnesses. For example, when anorexics engage in self-induced vomiting, they risk tearing the esophagus (the tube leading to the stomach) and destroying tooth enamel from acid in the vomit.

An anorexic person who misuses laxatives can suffer damage to the muscular function of the bowel. Laxative misuse also drains the body of water plus electrolytes that are essential for many body functions. Electrolytes exist in the blood and include minerals and salts such as sodium, calcium, potassium, chlorine, magnesium, and bicarbonate.

Low levels of electrolytes can affect the body in a variety of ways. A diet low in calcium, for one example, can lead to low bone mass density, which is the forerunner of osteoporosis, meaning "porous bones," that often results in bone fractures. Potassium deficiencies result in muscle weakness, irritability, apathy, drowsiness, mental confusion, and irregular heartbeat. Electrolyte imbalances can lead to edema, or a buildup of fluid in the body, usually in the legs and ankles.

Because an anorexic does not get enough food, her or his body may begin to feed off itself, causing a decrease in muscle mass, which results in weakness and low blood pressure. Respiratory infections, kidney failure, blindness, and heart disease are other risks.

A person afflicted with anorexia is likely to weigh 15 percent below what is considered normal for her or his age and height. Often, anorexic women do not menstruate for several months and, in some cases, may develop a growth of baby-fine hair (called lanugo) on her body, which may be a way for the body to conserve heat. Anorexics' nails may become brittle and their joints may swell.

Physical complications brought on by anorexia can kill. Between 10 and 20 percent of anorexics die from such medical problems as a weakened heart, kidney and liver damage, and depression, which can lead to suicide. As Judy Tam Sargent, a

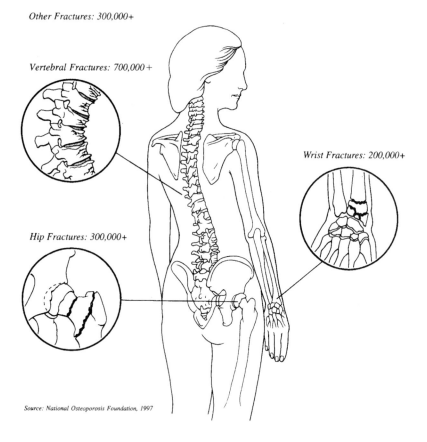

Other Fractures: 300,000+

Vertebral Fractures: 700,000+

Wrist Fractures: 200,000+

Hip Fractures: 300,000+

Source: National Osteoporosis Foundation, 1997

A diet low in calcium can result in osteoporosis, which means that bones can fracture easily.

mental health nurse, recovered anorexic, and author of *The Long Road Back: A Survivor's Guide to Anorexia* wrote: "Life with anorexia nervosa is a living nightmare. I wouldn't wish it upon my worst enemy."

Among the physical problems Sargent experienced was being "horribly cold" most of the time. She "became chronically depressed (even suicidal, at times), my bones became brittle . . . leading to a broken foot, several surgeries and eventually a joint fusion when nothing else worked . . . It was miserable."[9]

In a foreword to her book, Sargent notes that anorexia "begins insidiously, often in a young woman who is bright, talented, and ambitious. Gradually it alters her carefree life, draws her inward, and isolates her from her family and friends. . . . As she loses weight progressively her body withers, her emotions constrict, and her mind becomes strained."[10]

Excessive Exercise

Another sign of anorexic behavior is compulsive exercise. Psychiatrist Thomas Holbrook of Rogers Memorial ED Center in Wisconsin sometimes walked "for up to eight hours a day—and eventually limited his daily food intake to a single salad." He is six feet tall and in 1988, after twelve years of suffering from eating disorders, he weighed just 135 pounds. "I was terrified of being fat," he explained.[11]

An anorexic from California told how she struggled to be perfect in everything she did and hated to look at herself in the mirror because she did not like her body shape. She began to

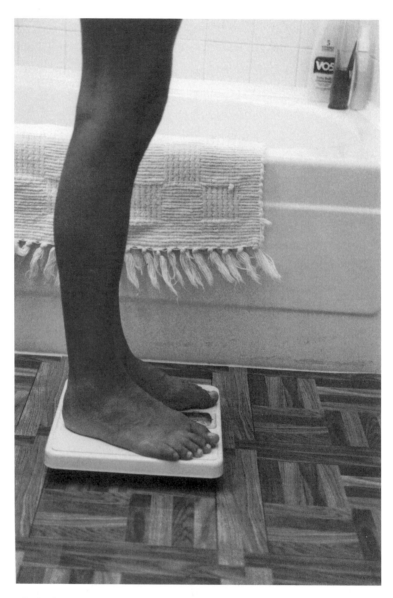

The bathroom scale is an all-important item in the life of someone with an eating disorder like anorexia or bulimia. Some people weigh themselves dozens of times a day to check for weight gain.

exercise compulsively, running five to six miles every day, sometimes wearing heavy sweats over plastic wrap around her body so she would perspire and thus lose water weight. After that, she would do 400 sit-ups every night.

Another teenager wrote about her anorexic pattern that began with a "healthy drive for success—in school, sports, and shape. It gradually led to an obsession that controls me twenty-four hours a day. . . . I became a compulsive exerciser, going to the gym for hours everyday, until the manager contacted my parents and warned them of the health risks involved."[12]

A regular exercise program is important for keeping in good health, but compulsive exercise can be a sign of anorexia.

While some gym trainers and fitness instructors are able to recognize compulsive exercisers, others may be drawn to these types of jobs because they themselves over exercise. They can justify long hours of working out, lifting weights, stair climbing, bike riding, or other physical activity as necessary to stay in shape. Instructors with obsessive exercise behavior can easily pass on their unhealthy attitudes about body image to those they train. An instructor who focuses on exercising to be thin rather than to be healthy is someone to stay away from, health experts warn.

Recognizing Bulimia

4

Because bulimia was not recognized as an illness until 1979, the symptoms, or signs, of the disorder were seldom taken seriously until about the mid-1980s. Karen Hamilton, a legal assistant in Florida, said that during the 1970s while in high school, she worked part time in a department store. One of her coworkers, who was about a year older, told Hamilton:

> how she and her boyfriend could eat anything they wanted and not gain weight. She said that in one night they ate pizza, snacks, and sundaes, and drank beer, then just made themselves throw up. She thought it was a great idea because she really liked to eat and said that she made herself throw up more times than her boyfriend. I remember thinking that there was no way I could force myself to throw up, but I thought she had a pretty good idea. I didn't

know until years later that there was a name for this and that it was a serious problem. Now, I wonder if her parents or doctors would have even known that she had an eating disorder.[1]

Even today, it is sometimes difficult to recognize a person with a bulimic disorder. Many bulimics maintain a fairly normal weight, primarily because between purging episodes some food stays in the digestive system, providing the body with some nutrients and calories.

Diagnosing Bulimia

Dentists are in a position to be among the first health-care professionals to detect bulimia. "Oral examinations . . . may reveal eroded teeth, fillings that are raised above the tooth surface, dry mouth, and related oral problems" indicating that the patient is bulimic, according to Roger Smith, DDS, dental director of Delta Dental Plan of Michigan.[2] In some cases, dentists can urge patients to get the psychological and medical help they need to recover.

The accepted criteria for diagnosing Bulimia Nervosa, as with Anorexia Nervosa, are stated in the DSM-IV:

A. Recurrent episodes of binge eating characterized by

1. Eating, in a discrete period of time (e.g., within any 2-hour period) an amount of food that is definitely larger than most people would eat under similar circumstances.

2. A sense of lack of control over eating during the episode (e.g., a feeling that one cannot stop eating or control what or how much one is eating).

B. Recurrent inappropriate compensatory behavior . . . to prevent weight gain, such as self-induced vomiting; misuse of laxatives, diuretics, enemas, or other medications; fasting; or excessive exercise. The binge eating and inappropriate compensatory behavior both occur, on average, at least twice a week for 3 months.

C. Self-evaluation is unduly influenced by body shape and weight.[3]

Bulimia nervosa usually starts in early adolescence, particularly among weight-conscious girls who diet, fail to lose a specified amount of weight, and react by binge eating. After bingeing, the bulimic purges by self-induced vomiting or by taking laxatives and/or diuretics to reduce fluids. According to various experts, bulimia patients average about fourteen episodes of binge-purging per week.

Physical Effects

Many of the physical effects associated with anorexics also affect bulimics. For example, gastric acid from self-induced vomiting causes tooth decay and deterioration of tooth enamel, an irreversible condition. Low levels of such minerals as calcium, phosphorus, and potassium can lead to fatigue, muscle spasms, or heart palpitations. Because bulimics often force themselves to vomit by sticking fingers or a toothbrush at the back of the throat, chronic throat irritation and "holes,"

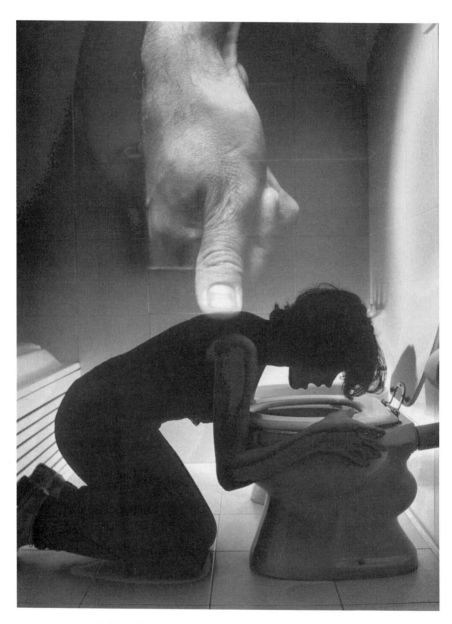

Bulimia is a force that controls the life of the sufferer.

or tears, in the esophagus may result. Frequent vomiting also causes swollen salivary glands, creating "chipmunk cheeks."

To induce vomiting, some bulimics take ipecac syrup, which is intended to be used as a remedy for accidentally ingesting certain poisons. But its repeated use is an especially dangerous practice. According to the National Institutes of Health (NIH), overdoses of ipecac can cause such side effects as "Diarrhea; fast or irregular heartbeat; nausea or vomiting (continuing for more than thirty minutes); stomach cramps or pain; troubled breathing; unusual tiredness or weakness; weakness, aching, and stiffness of muscles, especially those of the neck, arms, and legs." The NIH emphasizes that "Ipecac should not be used to cause vomiting as a means of losing weight. If used regularly for this purpose, serious heart problems or even death may occur."[4]

Digestive problems also occur among bulimics. One such danger is acid reflux, in which foods partially digested by acids and enzymes in the stomach involuntarily move back up into the esophagus. If this condition becomes chronic, the result can be damage to the esophagus, larynx, and lungs. There is even the danger of cancer developing.

Bulimics may also develop ulcers, or open sores, in the stomach. When bulimics do not ingest food for long periods of time the acid in an empty stomach begins to eat away at the lining. Too much food in the stomach for long periods of time also can damage the tissues.

People with Bulimia

Famous individuals who struggled with bulimia include not only Princess Diana of Wales, but also celebrities who in recent years have been able to share their experiences on the Web, in interviews for magazine and newspaper articles, in books, and on TV talk shows. Among them are musician Elton John; comedienne Joan Rivers; and actresses Jane Fonda, Barbara Niven, and Maria Conchita Alonso.

Alonso's bulimic condition began during the 1980s. Reportedly, her boyfriend constantly criticized her for being "fat," even though she was quite trim. She began dieting and lost enough weight to drop a dress size. In an interview for *People Magazine,* she told about a promotion trip to Mexico and finding a "huge bag of chocolate" in her hotel suite. She ate all the chocolate, then, she reported:

> I went crazy. I thought, "I can't gain any weight!" That's when I went to the bathroom and threw up. I had no idea there was a disease called bulimia. I thought, "This is so cool. I can eat something and then throw it up! Wow." I had no idea it could hurt me, so I started throwing up once every two or three days. Then it became once every day, then a couple of times a day. I was always in the bathroom.[5]

Alonso's bulimic behavior lasted for at least ten years. Purging caused damage to her esophagus and teeth. Fortunately, she got medical help and was able to restore her health. But, in her words, "bulimia is like alcoholism; you never get rid of it. . . . Right now the disorder is under control, but it's something I always think about. . . . I'll live with it forever."[6]

Musician Elton John struggled with bulimia.

Millions of other individuals who are not well known are addicted to binge eating and then purging. People find numerous ways to purge, usually keeping their practice hidden. A college student described how she binged and purged at home:

> Sometimes it would be late at night and my parents would be sleeping. I'd gorge myself with chips, leftover pizza, peanut butter and jelly sandwiches. It was like I couldn't chew fast enough. Then I'd go into the garage and line a paper grocery bag with a plastic one and use that as my toilet. I'd hide the bag until I could dispose of it.[7]

What Leads to Bulimia?

Experts repeatedly say there is no single cause for any eating disorder, and no one knows exactly what triggers bulimia. However, as with anorexia, biological factors may play a part. One of those factors is abnormal levels of neurotransmitters, or brain chemicals. High levels of the brain chemical serotonin, for example, can result in mood changes and loss of appetite. People with high serotonin levels also are likely to be obsessive and anxious.

Biologic factors may also be responsible for the binge-and-purge cycle. According to WebMD:

> Studies on animal behavior and prisoners of war suggest that chronic food restriction (such as severe dieting) often leads to a pattern of bingeing that persists even decades after regular food supplies are restored. . . . Some experts believe that the metabolism [the physical and chemical

processes involved in maintaining life] adapts to the bulimic cycle of bingeing and purging by slowing down, thereby increasing the risk of weight gain from even normal calorie intake. The process of vomiting and use of laxatives may stimulate the production of natural opioids—narcotics in the brain that cause an addiction to the bulimic cycle.[8]

Personality disorders can also contribute to bulimia. Some researchers have found that bulimics have a constant need for admiration. They usually cannot stand to be alone, are supersensitive to criticism or failure, and believe they can never live up to what is expected of them. Usually, people with eating disorders cannot distinguish between their negative thoughts about themselves and who they really are. "Everyone who has an eating disorder has terrible thoughts about themselves, but the thoughts lie," a young woman in Florida said.[9]

Sexual, physical, and verbal abuse are factors that lead some people to develop EDs. Survivors of abuse often try to numb their feelings of depression, helplessness, anger, or shame by starving, bingeing, and then purging.

Alcohol or other drug abuse may be related, as well. This type of abuse "occurs in one third of patients with bulimia nervosa," say the co-directors of the eating disorders clinic at the University of Kansas School of Medicine. "Thus, the substance abuse and the reasons for it must be addressed before effective treatment for bulimia nervosa can be initiated."[10]

In some cases, the stage may be set for bulimia early in life. Youngsters who have been teased by family members or classmates about their general appearance, such as the way they

Symptoms of Anorexia or Bulimia

Not all anorexics or bulimics exhibit the same set of symptoms. But here are some to consider:

Physical Symptoms

- Dramatic weight loss (at least 15 percent) over a short period of time with no medical illness diagnosed.
- Low body temperature.
- Dry hair or skin.
- Fine body hair (new growth of hair).
- Swollen ankles and feet.
- Erosion of tooth enamel.
- Amenorrhea (loss of menstrual period).
- Fatigue.

Behavioral Symptoms

- Avoiding social events where food will be present.
- Constantly talking about food, dieting, or weight loss, but denying hunger.
- Pretending to eat and throwing food away.
- Skipping meals and refusing to eat with others.
- Exercising for long periods of time.
- Going to the bathroom frequently.
- Wearing oversized clothes to hide a thin body.
- Exhibiting sadness and expressing feelings of worthlessness.
- Complaining about feeling fat.
- Feeling cold much of the time.

dress or their hairstyle, or about their weight and size, may be prone to unhealthy eating behaviors.

Physical changes in puberty, social pressures, transition to middle school or high school, and relationship problems with family members and friends also contribute to unhealthy attitudes toward food. Indiana teenager Brandie G. became bulimic at twelve years of age. Brandie said her eating disorder began because she "wanted to be perfect for her boyfriend." She thought she was overweight, so she decided to do something about her "problem." Instead of dieting or starving herself, she planned to get some food in her system, then dispose of it. For a time, Brandie thought she was "doing a real nice job" losing weight, but her friends had a different perspective.

One friend, Tasha, told Brandie that she was "really hurting herself." But Brandie insisted that she was fine, even though she suffered headaches, stomach pains, and other ailments. And no matter how hard Tasha tried to intervene, Brandie found a way to continue her damaging behavior.

Finally, Tasha realized that she could not help her friend by herself. She discussed Brandie's behavior with a teacher, who contacted a counselor. Throughout the school year, the counselor helped Brandie gain self-esteem and learn about the health dangers of bulimia. She gradually overcame her eating disorder. "One day I woke up and told myself that I was through," Brandie said. She began to eat regularly, and now is thankful for the help of Tasha, the teacher, and the counselor. Would she ever consider bulimic behavior again? "No," she said, "It's just not worth damaging your body trying to be perfect for someone else."[11]

5

Binge Eating Disorder

I t is not uncommon to hear someone admit that he or she just "pigged out on a box of chocolates" or "went on a binge, eating a half-gallon of ice cream while watching TV last night." Eating a lot of food at one time does not always mean that a person has an unhealthy attitude toward eating. Many people overeat on occasion, particularly during holidays or festivals when they make a conscious decision to overindulge. But someone with a binge eating disorder (BED) eats far more food than what most people could consume in the same time period. A person with BED may consume up to 20,000 calories during a binge episode, while a person who does not suffer from this disorder will normally consume between 2,000 and 3,000 calories per day, depending on a person's height, age, and physical characteristics.

One young woman with BED listed all the ingredients of a binge that lasted about two hours. It started with simply eating fried rice leftovers and led to eating quesadillas, eventually eating a block of cheddar cheese, a half box of cereal, a half gallon of milk, a loaf of white bread, a cup of butter and a cup of cinnamon sugar (for the bread), a box of brownie mix stirred up and eaten raw, and several cans of diet drink.

A case described in the *American Journal of Psychiatry* includes a similar "menu" during a typical binge by a woman with a long history of binge eating. The disorder began when she was about eleven years of age. The woman ingested:

The food on this table represents what a compulsive overeater might consume in about two hours.

two pieces of chicken, one small bowl of salad, two servings of mashed potatoes, one hamburger, one large serving of French fries, one fast-food serving of apple pie, one large chocolate shake, one large bag of potato chips, and between fifteen and twenty small cookies—all within a two-hour period.[1]

What Is BED?

Binge eating was first identified in 1959. Although it is not yet an official diagnosis, it is included as an "Eating Disorder Not Otherwise Specified" in the DSM-IV, the guidelines used by psychiatrists for making a diagnosis. It is also described in Appendix B of DSM-IV, which contains suggested categories for further research on this disorder.[2] Some ED experts believe it is the most common eating disorder and that a specific clinical designation and diagnostic criteria should be included in the manual just as they are for anorexia and bulimia.

Binge eating is defined as uncontrolled consumption of an unusually large quantity of food over a relatively short time period (within about two hours). It resembles bulimia nervosa and is often associated with the disease, but unlike bulimics, BED sufferers do not usually purge their bodies of excess food.[3]

A person who binges eats more rapidly than usual, eats large quantities of food when not physically hungry, eats alone, eats until uncomfortably full, and after a binge feels guilty or depressed. At least three or more of these conditions are part of a BED episode. In addition, episodes occur at least two days a week for six months. Binge eaters often are involved in a cycle of feeling emotionally upset, eating to neutralize the feelings, then getting upset for eating too much, and eating again to ease the pain.[4]

Many people who are binge eaters appear to be addicted to food, "using a bowl of pasta or a pound of M&Ms as a narcotic to stem the pain," as Tom put it in his story posted on a Web site. Food, to him, is "the friend that never fails."[5]

Who Suffers from BED?

According to the National Institutes of Health (NIH):

> about 2 percent of all adults in the United States (as many as four million Americans) have binge eating disorder. About 10 to 15 percent of people who are mildly obese and who try to lose weight on their own or through commercial weight-loss programs have BED. The disorder is even more common in people who are severely obese.[6]

Nevertheless, not all people who are obese are compulsive overeaters.

About 30 percent of people participating in medically supervised eating disorder programs suffer from binge eating, reports the National Women's Health Information Center (NWHIC) of the Office on Women's Health in the Department of Health and Human Services. BED is more common in women than in men, with three women affected for every two men. The disorder affects African Americans as often as

Caucasians, but its frequency in other ethnic groups is not yet known, according to NWHIC.

BED Causes

As is the case with other EDs, no one is certain what causes binge eating disorder. A major risk factor is negative self-evaluation, stemming from perfectionism or from self-hatred, sometimes brought on by sexual and physical abuse during childhood. One young woman, Maura, began to overeat when she was in seventh grade, explaining:

> It was a tough time for me (as it is for most girls)—physical development, social isolation, emotional imbalance. At this time, I began to look to my mother for guidance, but she was so wrapped up in her own problems that she had little or nothing to give. . . . Aside from being an alcoholic, she was a compulsive overeater herself. . . . I began to eat for comfort then, and gained weight as I was developing a woman's body. The taunts from my classmates at being slightly chubby led me to eat even more, and grow more and more fat. . . . [then] in eighth grade my self-loathing was increased a thousandfold when I was sexually abused by my brother. And so the cycle increased—food comforted me.[7]

Numerous studies and surveys have concluded that children who are the targets of taunts about their weight may develop psychological problems that can be factors in binge eating disorders.[8] "Large children and teens often live with vicious prejudice from classmates, parents and teachers, which can interfere with their ability to grow into self-assured, successful adults," wrote well-known nutritionist Frances M. Berg.[9]

Depression could be a factor in eating disorders, but it is not known whether depression leads to binge eating disorder or whether BED causes depression. Many people who are binge eaters say that being angry, ashamed, sad, bored, or worried can cause them to binge. Impulsive behavior (acting quickly without thinking) and certain other emotional problems appear to be more common in people with binge eating disorder.

The Obesity Dilemma

Because people with binge eating disorder do not purge themselves of food, they usually are obese—more than 20 percent above their healthy body weight.[10] But it is important to remember that obesity does not automatically indicate that a person is suffering from BED. An increasing number of Americans and people worldwide tend to be overweight or obese. In fact, in 1999, the United States Centers for Disease Control (CDC) released a long-term study showing that the number of overweight Americans is reaching epidemic proportions. One in five American adults is now considered obese, compared to about one in eight in the early 1990s.

Numerous government and private sector organizations are calling attention to the health issues associated with obesity, such as high cholesterol, high blood pressure, diabetes, gallbladder disease, heart disease, and some types of cancer.

Warning Signs

Stories from people with BED usually include early warning signs about their disorder. One of the behaviors that can signal a BED is a history of repeated dieting. Other BED warning signs and symptoms are:

- Gaining weight rapidly
- Fluctuating between weight gain and weight loss
- Eating large amounts of food without being hungry
- Eating an abnormal amount of food in a short period of time (usually less than two hours)
- Eating rapidly
- Lack of control—not able to stop eating
- Eating alone and hiding food
- Eating late at night
- Feeling disgust and shame after overeating
- Hoarding food (especially high calorie, junk food)
- Coping with emotional and psychological states such as stress, unhappiness, or disappointment by eating
- Consuming food to the point of being uncomfortable or even in pain
- Avoiding purge methods used by many bulimics
- Attributing successes and failures to weight
- Avoiding social situations, especially those involving food
- Being in an anxious or depressed mood

Some compulsive overeaters eat in secret or late at night.

Yet, the barrage of information about obesity has sometimes had a negative effect, creating even more fears about fat and reinforcement of prejudice against the obese. The pervasive fear of fat also leads to dangerous dieting practices and disordered eating. Children and adolescents are especially vulnerable.

There is debate among health care professionals regarding the reason for increasing obesity among young people. Heredity, inactivity, the kinds of foods eaten, and parents who encourage overeating are a few of the factors that contribute to the problem. "The bottom line," wrote nutritionist Frances Berg, "is that researchers and many health professionals now recognize obesity as a complex condition . . . there is much we don't know about childhood obesity—or what to do about it."[11]

In spite of the fact that obesity is a problem for BED patients, losing weight is usually not the first priority in overcoming the disorder. Rather, it is achieving normal eating behavior. Doctors and other health practitioners try to help patients establish a regular meal pattern and eliminate snacking, particularly before bedtime. By controlling binge episodes, some degree of weight loss usually occurs.

How are binge episodes controlled? One method is called cognitive behavior therapy. In this type of therapy, a BED patient is taught techniques for monitoring food habits and changing behavior and thought patterns.

Another method used is interpersonal psychotherapy, which focuses on improving relationships with family and friends. Because persons with BED often suffer from depression, antidepressant drugs are sometimes prescribed. In addition, self-help and support groups, such as Overeating Anonymous, provide techniques for treating BED, as do many ED treatment centers.

6

How Eating Disorders Are Treated

Treatment for eating disorders is seldom a simple matter. According to the United States Department of Health and Human Services (HHS), there is no universally accepted standard treatment. Ideally, there is a team approach to treatment, which would include the skills of a family physician, mental health professionals who help with emotional problems, and a nutritionist who can advise on a healthy diet. Various types of psychotherapy may be employed, including family and group therapy.

Psychotherapy plays a major role in treatment because people with eating disorders may be part of abusive or controlling families and have deep-seated emotional problems. An eating disorder often becomes a way to maintain control over oneself and her or his relationships. A sense of control also helps block out painful feelings and emotions. If events and emotions cannot be controlled, then at least the intake of food can be controlled, so the reasoning goes.

Controlling a need for food is also a way to escape stressful life events. The possibility of losing or giving up this mechanism is frightening for people with EDs and often prevents them from seeking help.

Getting Help

Some people recognize that they need help when they watch a TV show, read an article, or see a billboard or poster about EDs. In other instances, friends or family members may express concern and urge a person with an ED to get treatment. Sometimes ED sufferers take the initiative to get help when they realize their behavior has made them physically ill. They may feel they have pushed their bodies too far and will die if they continue to starve, binge and purge, or eat compulsively.

ED sufferers also may seek help after taking the Eating Attitudes Test (EAT-26). This test was developed by David M. Garner, director of the Toledo Center for Eating Disorders in Ohio, and his colleagues. Published in *Psychological Medicine* in 1982, EAT-26 is "probably the most widely used standardized measure of symptoms and concerns characteristic of eating disorders," according to Garner in a statement on the International Eating Disorder Referral Organization Web site. "Many studies have been conducted using the EAT-26 as a screening tool and are based on the assumption that early identification of an eating disorder can lead to earlier treatment,"[1]

Eating Attitude Test (EAT-26)

	Always	Very often	Often	Sometimes	Rarely	Never
1. Am terrified about being overweight.	❑	❑	❑	❑	❑	❑
2. Avoid eating when I am hungry.	❑	❑	❑	❑	❑	❑
3. Find myself preoccupied with	❑	❑	❑	❑	❑	❑
4. Have gone on eating binges where I feel that I may not be able to	❑	❑	❑	❑	❑	❑
5. Cut my food into small pieces.	❑	❑	❑	❑	❑	❑
6. Aware of the calorie content of foods that I eat.	❑	❑	❑	❑	❑	❑
7. Particularly avoid foods with a high carbohydrate content (e.g. bread, potatoes, rice, etc.).	❑	❑	❑	❑	❑	❑
8. Feel that others would prefer if I ate more.	❑	❑	❑	❑	❑	❑
9. Vomit after I have eaten.	❑	❑	❑	❑	❑	❑
10. Feel extremely guilty after eating.	❑	❑	❑	❑	❑	❑
11. Am preoccupied with a desire to be thinner.	❑	❑	❑	❑	❑	❑
12. Think about burning up calories when I exercise.	❑	❑	❑	❑	❑	❑
13. Other people think that I am too thin.	❑	❑	❑	❑	❑	❑
14. Am preoccupied with the thought of having fat on the body.	❑	❑	❑	❑	❑	❑
15. Take longer than others to eat my meals.	❑	❑	❑	❑	❑	❑
16. Avoid foods with sugar in them.	❑	❑	❑	❑	❑	❑
17. Eat diet foods.	❑	❑	❑	❑	❑	❑
18. Feel that food controls my life.	❑	❑	❑	❑	❑	❑
19. Display self control around food.	❑	❑	❑	❑	❑	❑
20. Feel that others pressure me to eat.	❑	❑	❑	❑	❑	❑
21. Give too much time and thought to food.	❑	❑	❑	❑	❑	❑
22. Feel uncomfortable after eating sweets.	❑	❑	❑	❑	❑	❑
23. Engage in dieting behavior.	❑	❑	❑	❑	❑	❑
24. Like my stomach to empty.	❑	❑	❑	❑	❑	❑
25. Enjoy trying new rich foods.	❑	❑	❑	❑	❑	❑
26. Have the impulse to vomit after meals.	❑	❑	❑	❑	❑	❑

Calculation of the scores: Always: 3 points; **Very often:** 2 points; **Often:** 1 point; **Others:** 0 point
Score of 0-10 points: Generally normal; Score of 11-20 points: You have tendency towards anorexia or bulimia; Score above 20 points: You are at high risk.

which helps reduce physical health risks and life-threatening conditions. The test has been posted on several Web sites. But Dr. Garner pointed out in an online conference that "A professional evaluation is essential, particularly a professional who has experience in the diagnosis and treatment of eating disorders."[2] Thus, to determine whether treatment is necessary, one of the first considerations should be consulting with a qualified specialist. A medical referral service can help locate such a person.

Information is also available from such organizations as the International Eating Disorder Referral Organization, the International Association of Eating Disorder, or the Renfrew Center's National Referral Network (see For More Information). These organizations, as well as many others that focus on helping people with EDs, also maintain Web sites.

ED Treatment Centers

Treatment for EDs frequently takes place on an outpatient basis, usually a day program in a hospital, clinic, or ED center. At one center, the Avalon Eating Disorder Treatment Centers in the Greater Buffalo, New York, area, a five-week treatment program is offered Monday through Friday for five hours each day. A primary therapist assesses each patient, monitors progress, and provides support and one-on-one psychotherapy. Group therapy involves peer support and addresses such issues as self-esteem, body image, and managing anger.

Although some people with EDs may appear to be on the road to recovery after outpatient therapy and medical treatment, they sometimes resume their compulsive eating behavior within a few days, weeks, or months. "When the eating disorder is severe or chronic, the optimal treatment setting is residential [live-in] care, where there can be intensive therapy in a setting that feels safe and is appropriately supportive, over a sufficient period of time," wrote psychiatrist Thomas Holbrook, director of the ED Center at Rogers Memorial Hospital in Wisconsin.[3]

The first residential facility for the treatment of eating disorders in the United States, the Renfrew Center, was established in Philadelphia, Pennsylvania, in 1985. Since then, Renfrew has set up treatment centers for women with eating disorders and other related mental health problems in New York City; Coconut Creek and Miami, Florida; northern New Jersey; southern Connecticut; and Bryn Mawr and Bucks County, Pennsylvania.

Numerous other treatment centers are scattered across the United States. Some are associated with universities or hospitals, such as the Harvard Eating Disorder Center in Massachusetts; the Rutgers Eating Disorders Clinic in New Jersey; Johns Hopkins Hospital Eating and Weight Disorders Program in Maryland; the Eating and Weight Disorders Program of the University of Iowa Hospital and Clinics; and the DePaul Tulane Behavioral Health Center Eating Disorders Program in Louisiana.

In-Patient Treatment

People who need in-patient care, either in a residential treatment center or hospital, often express the kind of terror that Diana K., who suffered an eating disorder, described in an online conference:

> I was scared out of my mind. I didn't know what to expect. . . . I didn't want to be there, but I knew deep inside I had to be. . . . When you get there, it's different from what you might imagine. It was a very nice place. Clean, very residential, like home.[4]

Creative arts therapy is part of the complex treatment utilized at the Renfrew Center in helping women and adolescent girls with eating disorders.

What goes on during the day at a treatment center? Simply put, the day is structured from morning through evening. Group therapy at specified times deals with setting realistic goals, identifying and expressing feelings, and learning how to eat with nutrition in mind. Individual and family therapy are a part of the day. Most programs allow time for self-expression through journal writing and various art forms.

The length of time residents stay at treatment centers varies. An average stay can range from several weeks to six months or more. In the opinion of Dr. Craig Johnson, director of the Eating Disorders Program at the highly respected Laureate Psychiatric Hospital in Tulsa, Oklahoma:

> The necessary length of stay to minimally restore normal weight for patients with anorexia nervosa is about sixty days. Patients with more severe bulimia who have not responded to informed outpatient interventions often require stays in the forty-five-day range.[5]

7
Treatment and Recovery Costs

At least 1,000 deaths occur each year because of anorexia, and several thousand die of multiple causes that are linked to anorexia and bulimia. However, if treatment begins at the first signs of an eating disorder, about 60 percent of ED sufferers recover within a short period of time. Without early treatment, recovery from EDs often takes years, and may require hospitalization or inpatient treatment in an ED center. Afterward, psychotherapy and medication may be needed.

No statistics have been gathered yet that measure the annual total costs of eating disorders to American society. However, because of the nation's obsession with thinness, the USFDA estimated the total cost of diet-related illnesses, which include depression, hair loss, heart attacks, strokes, anorexia, and bulimia, is about $140 billion a year.[1]

ED Treatment Costs

Costs for treating EDs range from a few thousand dollars to tens of thousands of dollars, depending on the time needed to recover. A person with an ED may have to fight the disease for a lifetime, just as an alcoholic or other drug abuser has to guard against giving in to his or her addiction. Healing Connections, Inc., a nonprofit organization that provides financial assistance for people who cannot afford treatment for EDs, notes that:

> On average, it takes two or three hospitalizations with long-term follow-up care to recover from an eating disorder. The average length of stay for someone requiring inpatient hospitalization is seven days, and the costs run between $4,900 and $7,000 per hospitalization (according to insurance standards). Day treatment . . . a way to prevent an inpatient stay, can cost between $4,500 and $9,000 for fifteen days. Medication costs range between $100 and $150 per month. Outpatient therapy costs between $45 and $125 per session.[2]

Few Insurance Benefits

Some health insurance policies cover part of the expenses of ED treatments, but benefits are usually limited to a set time period. In addition, most treatment centers require an initial deposit or total payment in advance, with the insured persons responsible for being reimbursed by their insurers. In some cases, this may require a family to borrow money or use up savings, or even sell a home to raise the funds.

Insurance benefits for eating disorders are not equal to those paid for other mental health and physical problems. For years, the National Association of Anorexia Nervosa and Associated Eating Disorders (ANAD) and other groups have been campaigning to eliminate discrimination against people with eating disorders by insurance companies, managed care, health management organizations (HMOs), and other health care providers. ANAD supports federal legislation that will require group health plans to offer the same type of mental health benefits, including coverage for eating disorders, that insurance companies provide for medical treatments.

ANAD also will help families with legal issues related to accessing care for EDs. The organization says it will suggest strategies for dealing with insurance discrimination and:

> provide lawyers to read any policy or contract and advise insurees on the extent of their mental health coverage. If an insuree brings a lawsuit against an insurance company . . . ANAD will provide pertinent supporting information and locate distinguished health professionals to advise lawyers and appear as expert witnesses.[3]

Emotional Costs

No dollar amount can ever convey the emotional costs of eating disorders—frustration, disappointment, disgust, pain, misery, worry, and fear. Seventeen-year old Alicia Khoo told of her "four years of purgatory." From her thirteenth through her sixteenth year, she struggled with anorexia and bulimia. Like many young girls, she became obsessed with thinness because, she says, a boyfriend told her she was "a little too fat." Yet, she says:

> in retrospect, I realize I was the most normal-looking girl you could find, healthy and all, within the acceptable weight range, and I did not look fat at all. But something inside me exploded, and then, a nightmare started, which I have only just recently fought and overcome successfully. I understand that had I sought professional help promptly, it would have ended earlier.

Alicia's "nightmare" included a period when she:

> wanted desperately to be attractive, thus I exercised and exercised, and detested food so much that eating was a chore, torture in fact, and then one day when my waistline was twenty-three inches instead of the original twenty-eight, I thought, "Ok, now I can 'treat' myself," which was weird, considering how successfully I had psyched myself into hating food.

Alicia then began a binge-and-purge pattern similar to those described by many other bulimics.

> I shudder recalling my extreme lack of control . . . I even contemplated ending my life. I felt ugly, disgusting, hateful . . . and there wasn't really anyone I could turn to, not even my mother, who suffered from severe bulimia and still does.

Alicia eventually consulted a counselor; she has been through numerous therapy sessions and involved in "plenty of self-analysis and self help." She also has received support from other members of her family and friends. She suffered relapses and once again became "totally obsessed with food." But one day she realized what was triggering her bulimic behavior: her skirts with twenty-three-inch waistlines! She was pressuring herself to fit into a skirt size that she wore when she was thirteen years old. So, in her words, she:

> took a practical, common-sense step and bought skirts with a larger waistline. I can't believe I actually tried squeezing, literally, into that punishing [skirt] for two years, and that's why I felt so miserable. I'm not supposed to fit my clothes, my clothes are supposed to fit me!

Alicia admits it took far too long to understand this simple logic. Now her advice to other ED sufferers is: "Do yourself a gigantic favor and seek help—now."[4]

Those who suffer from EDs are not alone in the emotional burdens inflicted. Family, friends, associates, classmates, and others are affected. The toll on parents of anorexics and bulimics can be extremely high. Some parents may feel guilty because of their children's condition and believe they have failed their offspring in some way. When they seek treatment for their children, parents frequently say they get frantic trying to find out what to do. They may also have financial worries when confronted with high treatment costs for their dependent children.

A tape measure can have a significant impact on a person who is addicted to being thin, but it does not measure the worth of that person.

Friends of people with eating disorders also face emotional ordeals. For example, Ralph Kopald, a personal physical trainer in California, has worked with a young woman, "Marsha," who has diabetes, a disease in which the body does not produce enough insulin. Kopald did "quite a bit of research" on what type of diet and training would be appropriate for Marsha, and presented her with an eating plan. But:

> when we started to go over it one afternoon, she stated she
> was getting nauseous simply reading the quantities and
> frequency [of eating] I was recommending. I asked if she
> ever had an eating disorder. Yep. Later I asked if she had

discussed her eating patterns or workout routine with her doctor. She had not."

So, Kopald explained to her that he would "prefer to work as part of a team—the doctor, his nutritionist, and me. That never happened."[5]

Kopald considers Marsha a good friend, and is extremely frustrated and saddened because he cannot convince her to seek skilled professional help. Yet Marsha continues to ask for Kopald's advice, and he will no doubt be persistent in encouraging Marsha to talk to her doctor.

Along with friends and family, there are many other individuals and groups working diligently to help people with eating disorders. They find ways to create awareness of eating disorders and call attention to programs that help ED sufferers recover.

8

Awareness and Prevention Programs

To create ED awareness and to help prevent the disorders, two faculty members of the University of California system, Kathryn Sylva and Robin Lasser, have used their graphic and photographic skills to create a dramatic visual arts project called "Eating Disorders in a Disordered Culture." The project is designed for gallery exhibition, public art spaces such as billboards and bus shelters, and the Internet.

Sylva and Lasser began their efforts in 1996, after Lasser revealed a long-held secret: As a young child, she was anorexic; at the age of twelve, she starved herself to a mere thirty-nine pounds. Lasser was hospitalized and eventually recovered, but her experience, which she shared years later with her friend, prompted the two to develop their public art and Web site project. One of their billboards sitting along Interstate 80 in California during October and November 1998 showed two outdoor grills aflame, with a message formed in sizzling ground meat: "Fear of Fat Eats Us Alive." On the billboard were the words "Some women don't just diet. They die. Anorexia Nervosa."

Their displays have appeared across the United States. In January and February 2001, the women presented a solo exhibit of "Eating Disorders in a Disordered World" at the gallery of the Parsons School of Design in New York City. In addition, graphics from the show were on billboards and banners in subway stations.

University of California faculty members, Robin Lasser and Kathryn Sylva, created an exhibition called "Eating Disorders in a Disordered Culture," which included exhibits in art galleries, posters, and billboard art. The billboard shown here stood along Interstate 80 in California during October and November, 1998.

Wherever the exhibit is featured, a central focus is a table carved with the words "secret appetites." On it are black plates etched with the words of anorexics, bulimics, and compulsive overeaters. Recorded first-person accounts reveal how ED sufferers and the people close to them have been affected. Those who see the show are invited to comment in writing, and their responses indicate the value of this type of public education. As one viewer wrote: "It helps so much to know that I am not alone." Another: "Thank you for opening up the issues and the feelings for those of us—like myself—who don't—or didn't—have a clue. I am beginning to understand."[1]

National Eating Disorders Awareness and Screening

Eating Disorders Awareness and Prevention (EDAP), founded in 1987, is one of the national nonprofit organizations that is dedicated to the prevention of eating disorders. A major organization effort is the Eating Disorders Awareness Week (EDAW) held in February each year. During that week, thousands of events are staged across the United States.

One event is a Body Fair. These fairs have been held at high schools in California, using a variety of presentations and interactive booths to inform students about the manipulative power of the media, the dangers of dieting, and weight discrimination. Such fairs also have promoted respect and appreciation for the natural diversity of body shapes and sizes. Art exhibits have been displayed in malls and community centers. Workshops to help change attitudes about unhealthy male images in the media have been conducted during the week, as well.

During the annual awareness week and other times during the year, EDAP conducts screening programs at high schools and colleges, where eating disorders are common. Hundreds of schools take part in the program, which began in 1996 on 600 college campuses; high school screening began in 2000. The program includes educational materials on eating disorders, opportunities to meet with health professionals, and information on how to encourage friends or family members to seek treatment for eating disorders.

One successful media protest in 1999 occurred in Sioux Falls, South Dakota, where a TV station used a billboard ad to promote the TV show, "Friends." The advertisement featured Jennifer Aniston, Courteney Cox Arquette, and Lisa Kudrow of "Friends" along with the words: "Cute anorexic chicks."

Angry Sioux Falls citizens demanded that the NBC affiliate KDLT immediately discontinue the billboard. Within a few days, the slogan on the billboard was changed. EDAP pointed out that the billboard glamorizing anorexia was an extreme example of ads that promote harmful body ideals, but it also showed that consumers can play a powerful role in changing media images.

Advertisers can also play constructive roles. Kellogg of Canada, Ltd., for example, conducted an unusual campaign in 1996 and 1997 to encourage healthy body images and to promote its Special K cereal. Advertising placed in magazines and

Media Watchdog Project

Another EDAP program is a media watchdog project. It encourages media viewers to take action when they see TV commercials, magazine ads, or billboards that promote thin body ideals, advising viewers to:

- Write a letter to an advertiser you think is sending positive, inspiring messages that recognize and celebrate the natural diversity of human body shapes and sizes. Compliment their courage to send positive, affirming messages.

- Tear out the pages of your magazines that contain advertisements or articles that glorify thinness or degrade people of larger sizes. Enjoy your magazine without negative media messages about your body.

- Talk to your friends about media messages and the way they make you feel.

- Make a list of companies who consistently send negative body image messages and make a conscious effort to avoid buying their products. Write them a letter explaining why you are using your "buying power" to protest their messages.[2]

on television attacked the fashion industry's ultra-thin beauty ideal.

One advertisement pictured a tape measure and began with the words: "It's unfortunate that something as insignificant as a tape measure can have such an impact on how we feel about ourselves. Don't let it. It can't measure who you are. Exercise. Refuse to skip meals. Start with a balanced breakfast every morning and go from there." It went on to describe the nutritional benefits of Kellogg's Special K cereal and to counsel viewers that "the standards you measure yourself by should be your own."

To people suffering from eating disorders, it may seem as though books and magazines bombard them with images of "perfect" bodies.

Another Kellogg advertisement depicted an unnaturally thin model in a bikini who looked as though she had been a prisoner of war. The copy read: "If this is beauty, there's something wrong with the eye of the beholder," and told the viewer that "a healthy body weight should be beautiful in anyone's eyes."[3]

Proposed Federal Legislation

Raising awareness of EDs in U.S. schools is the purpose of a United States Congressional bill proposed in 2000 and again in 2001. Called the Eating Disorders Awareness, Prevention, and Education Act of 2001 (H.R. 46), the law would amend the Elementary and Secondary Education Act of 1965. Its purpose is:

> (1) To provide States, local school districts, and parents with the means and flexibility to improve awareness of, identify, and help students with eating disorders; (2) To help ensure that such individuals receive a quality education and secure their chance for a bright future.

The bill also calls for:

> . . . programs to improve the identification of students with eating disorders, increase awareness of such disorders among parents and students, and train educators (such as teachers, school nurses, school social workers, coaches, school counselors, and administrators) on effective eating disorder prevention and assistance methods.

85

If passed, the Act would require the secretary of the U.S. Department of Education to consult with the Department of Health and Human Services and the National Institutes of Health and develop a program to improve public awareness and prevention of eating disorders. Finally, the National Center for Education Statistics and the National Center for Health Statistics would be required to "conduct a study on the impact eating disorders have on educational advancement and achievement." The study would:

> (1) evaluate the extent to which students with eating disorders are more likely to miss school, have delayed rates of development, or have reduced cognitive [reasoning] skills;
>
> (2) report on current State and local programs to educate youth about the dangers of eating disorders, as well as evaluate the value of such programs; and
>
> (3) make recommendations on measures that could be undertaken by Congress, the Department of Education, States, and local educational agencies to strengthen eating disorder prevention and awareness programs.[4]

School Efforts

Some ED educational materials are already being used in schools. In some classrooms, videotapes provide a basis for discussions about EDs. One video, *Self-Image: The Fantasy, The Reality* from the popular PBS program *In the Mix* for teenagers, focuses on how media images drive teenagers to diet constantly, use anabolic steroids, and to develop eating disorders. The program helps spark class discussions about unrealistic body images presented in the media and the importance of developing self-confidence and personal style.

Another video, *Afraid to Eat: Eating Disorders and the Student-Athlete*, was produced by the National Collegiate Athletic Association. The video uses interviews with student athletes, coaches, and medical personnel to define anorexia and bulimia and describe the consequences of eating disorders.

In recent years, numerous curriculum materials for junior high and high school classrooms have been published. An example is a twelve-week course prepared by EDAP called *Go Girls!* It was first used in the high schools of the Seattle, Washington, area in 1998. Since then students in high schools and middle schools in more than one hundred cities in nine states have participated.

Students write an essay about why they want to attend a *Go Girls!* class. Those chosen meet once a week and learn how to voice their opinions about the lack of body-shape diversity in the media, entertainment, and fashion industries. They make presentations to executives at retail corporations, write letters to national advertisers, participate in TV and radio interviews, and conduct campaigns in local high schools. One high school mentor said the girls involved developed greater self-esteem, learned to accept "diversity of body sizes," and increased their "sense of empowerment."[5]

Another set of classroom materials is titled "The Eating Concerns Support Group Curriculum" for grades seven through twelve by Thomas J. Shiltz of the Rogers Memorial

Hospital in Wisconsin. It is designed to help students achieve healthy lifestyles. School personnel receive training in how to lead a support group. Students who participate in the group meet once a week for twelve weeks during the school day, taking part in discussions about eating disorders, learning how EDs develop and can be overcome. During the course, students focus on activities that cover such topics as healthy eating, expressing feelings, reducing stress, and recognizing and affirming their strengths.

Curriculum materials also are available from the Office on Women's Health of the United States Department of Health and Human Services. The *BodyWise Eating Disorders Information Packet for Middle School Personnel* can be ordered by mail from HHS or can be downloaded from the Internet (see Internet Addresses). All the materials can be freely reproduced.

Included in the packet are information sheets for school personnel, parents, and students. A student sheet explains how to help a friend who shows signs of having an eating disorder:

- Do not keep your suspicions to yourself.
- Tell your friend you are concerned about his or her behavior, such as not eating or vomiting after lunch.
- Encourage your friend to talk to a teacher, school nurse, counselor, or parent.
- Talk to a trusted older person who can get help for your friend.

These actions may seem familiar. Tasha, described earlier, took similar steps to help her friend, Brandie, find the road to recovery.

Classroom reading is also an excellent way to learn about and discuss eating disorders. *The Best Little Girl in the World,* first published in 1978, for example, is a classic young adult novel dealing with anorexia. Written by Steven Levenkron, a therapist and ED authority, the book has been republished and is often used to create awareness about EDs. Other more recent works of nonfiction on the topic are listed in Further Reading.

9

Current and Future Research

Cheryl, who began binge-and-purge cycles when she was fifteen years old, was still bulimic twelve years later when she took part in a study at the University of Minnesota. The study, which was published in 2000, was designed to determine whether a drug to prevent nausea after chemotherapy for cancer would be an effective treatment for bulimia. Along with Cheryl, thirteen other women took the drug ondansetron (sold as Zofran) while twelve others were given a placebo, a pill with no medication in it.

After a month, the women receiving Zofran had about half the number of binge-purge episodes a week than those getting the placebo. For Cheryl, the effect was even more dramatic. She reported that "Within two days of taking the medicine, the symptoms disappeared. I did not have a reduction in symptoms; I had complete remission."[1] However, the author of the study, Patricia L. Faris, Ph.D., emphasized that ondansetron is not a cure for bulimia, and further experiments are needed. Along with taking the drug, participants in an expanded study receive psychotherapy, which some experts believe reduces bulimic behavior even more than the drug does. Long-term effects of Zofran are still unknown.

Clinical Trials

The experiment in which Cheryl was a participant is one of several clinical trials, or research studies, attempting to determine how best to treat eating disorders. Clinical trials are usually conducted after researchers test their ideas or procedures in the laboratory. If these test results are promising, researchers begin the first phase of experiments involving a small number of volunteer patients. Later phases involve larger numbers of participants to test the effectiveness of a drug or treatment.

The United States government has strict guidelines and safeguards to protect people who choose to participate in clinical trials. Every clinical trial in the United States must be approved and monitored by an Institutional Review Board to make sure the risks are as low as possible and are worth any potential benefits.

Some research is sponsored by the U.S. National Institutes of Health (NIH). NIH has developed ClinicalTrials.gov, a Web site that provides current information about clinical research studies.

The site describes a clinical trial under way at the New York State Psychiatric Institute to determine the effectiveness of treating bulimia nervosa with an antidepressant medication, fluoxetine, and with behavior therapy. A patient has to meet the DSM-IV criteria for bulimia nervosa and be a female at least eighteen years old. Treatment lasts for four months, and during that time, a patient visits a health-care center about once a week for the first month, and then usually once every other week for the remaining three months.

Another study, by the Eating Disorders Clinic at Stanford University in California, is designed to compare two different outpatient treatments for women (ages fourteen to fifty) who currently have anorexia nervosa, or who have had anorexia nervosa in the recent past. Treatment for one group involves medication therapy and education on medication management; treatment for the second group includes medication as well as behavioral and family therapy.

Future Drugs

Will the drug Zofran, which Cheryl believed helped in her recovery from bulimia, become widely used to treat this disorder? It is a question that can only be answered after future trials and experiments.

Another question awaiting a future answer focuses on the theory behind the drug's use. The Minnesota researchers, who studied its effects for ten years before clinical trials began, believe that bingeing and vomiting over months or years can damage the nervous system, particularly the vagus nerve, which controls satiety, or the feeling of being full after eating. Repeated vomiting is, as Dr. Faris explained, a "jolt to the vagus, and the vagus gets used to this really intense stimulation. It then begins to cycle in patterns of increased activity. When activity in the vagus nerve becomes hyperactive, that is interpreted as the urge to engage in bulimic behaviors."[2]

The drug being studied decreases abnormal vagal activity and suggests to researchers that there is a physiological factor in bulimia that can be corrected. Not all experts agree, however, contending that the theory is difficult if not impossible to

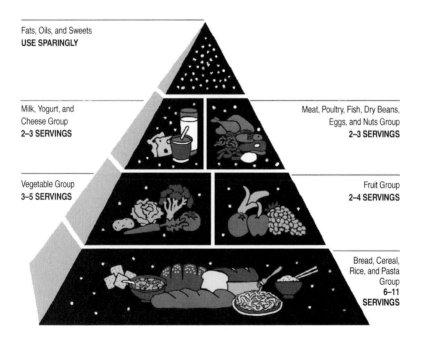

Fats, Oils, and Sweets
USE SPARINGLY

Milk, Yogurt, and Cheese Group
2–3 SERVINGS

Meat, Poultry, Fish, Dry Beans, Eggs, and Nuts Group
2–3 SERVINGS

Vegetable Group
3–5 SERVINGS

Fruit Group
2–4 SERVINGS

Bread, Cereal, Rice, and Pasta Group
6–11 SERVINGS

Eating with nutrition in mind is important for everyone, but it is a primary goal for anyone recovering from an eating disorder. The USDA Food Guide Pyramid for daily eating is shown above.

prove and that psychotherapy and antidepressant medication have greater success rates. In addition, the drug therapy treats a physical symptom, not the underlying psychological problems that may have triggered bulimia.

Another medication that could be used in the future to treat an eating disorder is topiramate. The drug was approved by the FDA in 1996 to control epileptic seizures. In clinical trials for the drug, researchers found that it suppressed appetite. This led Nathan Shapira and other researchers at the University of Cincinnati (Ohio) to undertake a small study of thirteen female patients with binge eating disorders. The women ranged in age from nineteen to fifty-four. All were prescribed Topamax, the trade name for topiramate.

The study's lead author Shapira, currently at the University of Florida in Gainesville, reported in 1999 that nine of the women decreased the number of binge-eating episodes and four completely ended their uncontrolled eating. He cautioned, however, that larger studies are needed to verify the drug's effectiveness.[3]

In 1998, researchers at the University of Texas Southwestern Medical Center identified a pair of hormones called orexin A and B that may help anorexics. During laboratory experiments, "researchers injected the hormones into rats' brains, [and] the animals ate eight to ten times more food than normal within a few hours," according to a report in *Science World*."[4] A team of scientist s headed by Masashi Yanagisawa hope that a drug can be developed to mimic orexin, which could increase the appetites of anorexics and persuade them to eat.

More Unanswered Questions

Whatever the clinical trials and current studies, many questions still remain unanswered regarding eating disorders. But future efforts no doubt will deal with such issues as these: What effects do stress and depression have on eating? How do physical and sexual abuse relate to eating disorders and obesity? What roles do biology, culture, and family play in the development and course of eating disorders? How can health-care practitioners determine what triggers the onset of anorexia or bulimia?

In the meantime, as researchers seek definitive answers to these questions, it is important to stress that recovery from eating disorders is possible. While treatment may vary with individuals, the first step for anyone struggling with an ED is getting help from an experienced mental-health professional before serious medical problems occur.

Q&A

Q. Are eating disorders contagious? Can I catch these diseases?

A. No. Eating disorders are not like the common cold or flu. You cannot "catch" these diseases. They are conditions that develop because of complex factors, including emotional, biological, and relationship problems.

Q. Many of my classmates try to look like their favorite TV or movie star. Is that healthy?

A. No. Most entertainment idols are not the perfect ideals they portray in the unrealistic images they present. Some have become anorexic or bulimic in order to maintain their idealized shapes, and they have damaged their health in the process. Trying to look like or be like someone you are not frequently leads to frustration and even despair, and can contribute to an eating disorder. "Be true to yourself" is age-old advice and applies to accepting your body shape and size.

Q. Do genes have anything to do with eating disorders?

A. Experts are trying to determine whether genes are a factor in eating disorders. If several of your family members have eating disorders, this could indicate that you might be prone to developing anorexia or bulimia. But other factors can put you at risk, such as a mother, father, or other family member who is overly critical about your weight. Abnormal brain chemical functions and cultural factors also can effect whether someone develops an eating disorder.

Q. I've heard that only a stupid person would want to starve on purpose. Do young people who become anorexic have lower than average intelligence?

A. No. In general, most anorexics are, or were, good students. They often are intelligent and hardworking, and tend to strive for perfection.

Q. After months of treatment, I have recovered from an eating disorder, but I'm worried about a relapse. What should I do?

A. Outpatient follow-up is extremely important. Stay in contact with your treatment program and, if possible, attend support group meetings. The support of your family, friends, and others is also an important part of ongoing recovery. Talk to someone you can trust whenever you have the urge to revert to your obsessive behavior. If you should binge, purge, or overeat, do not punish yourself. Remember that recovery is an ongoing process.

Q. Just about everyone I know is on some kind of diet or is talking about dieting. Is dieting really dangerous?

A. In many cases, dieting to change your body shape and size, as opposed to eating in a healthy manner, can be dangerous. Dieting rarely works because most people regain whatever weight they have lost within one to five years. Those who repeat cycles of dieting and regaining weight are at increased risk for health problems such as heart disease. Chronic dieting can weaken muscles, create stress and anxiety, decrease your energy level, and disrupt your ability to concentrate.

Q. What is a healthy way to eat?

A. The basis of a healthy eating pattern is the USDA's Food Guide Pyramid. To make sure you get enough nutrients, make food choices from each major group in the Pyramid, and eat regular meals in a relaxed atmosphere. Enjoy what you eat, rather than constantly fussing about how food will affect your weight.

Timeline

1380—Saint Catherine of Siena, who starves and punishes herself to prove her holiness, dies at the age of thirty-three.

1694—Richard Morton's *Phthisiologia: or a Treatise of Consumptions* is published. It describes a twenty-year-old female whom he treated for symptoms similar to those of anorexia nervosa.

1873—London physician Sir William Gull identifies and names anorexia nervosa.

1980—Bulimia nervosa is described as a symptom of an eating disorder in the third edition of the American Psychiatric Association's standard reference guide, *The Diagnostic and Statistical Manual of Mental Disorders.*

1983—Entertainer Karen Carpenter dies of complications due to anorexia, calling public attention to the disease for the first time.

1987—A nonprofit organization, Eating Disorders Awareness and Prevention, Inc., is founded in Seattle, Washington.

1992—The Women's Task Force of the American College of Sports Medicine describes the "Female Athlete Triad," which refers to the interrelated risks of disordered eating, menstrual dysfunction, and osteoporosis among female athletes.

1994—Gymnast Christy Henrich dies at age twenty-two of multiple organ failure, the result of anorexia.

2000 –2001—The Eating Disorders Awareness, Prevention, and Education Act is introduced in the U. S. House of Representatives.

Glossary

anabolic steroids—Drugs taken to become bigger and stronger, enhance athletic performance, and improve physical appearance.

anxiety—Great apprehension, or the vague feeling that something terrible is about to happen.

chemotherapy—Using drugs to destroy cancer cells.

cognitive—The process of knowing, reasoning, and being aware.

compensatory behavior—Behavior that offsets previous actions.

culture—Learned behavior patterns, arts, beliefs, institutions, and other aspects of a specific population.

depression—A psychotic condition characterized by an inability to concentrate, insomnia, and feelings of dejection and guilt.

diuretic—Tending to increase the discharge of urine.

electrolytes—Minerals in body tissues which, when dissolved in water, may become electrically charged particles controlling the movement of the body's nutrients and waste.

fasting—Eating very little or abstaining from food for a set period.

flagellation—Beating oneself or another person for "purification."

harassment—Behavior that annoys, worries, or threatens another.

heart palpitations—Temporary irregular heartbeats sometimes accompanied by light-headedness and/or shortness of breath.

hormone—A substance naturally produced in the body that regulates varied functions.

martyr—One who suffers great pain and death for a cause.

osteoporosis—A disease characterized by low bone mass and deterioration of bone tissue.

placebo—A substance that looks like a drug but contains no medication.

psychotherapy—Using psychological methods to treat mental and emotional disorders.

syndrome—A set of signs and symptoms occurring together to characterize a physical or mental health problem.

synthetic—Not genuine; artificial; devised.

For More Information

Academy for Eating
Disorders (AED)
6728 Old McLean Village
Drive
McLean, VA 22101
(703) 556-9222
http://www.acadeatdis.org

American Anorexia/Bulimia
Association (AABA)
165 W. 46th St.
Suite 1108
New York, NY 10036
(212) 575-6200
http://www.aabainc.org

Eating Disorder Referral and
Information Center
International Eating
Disorder Referral
Organization
2923 Sandy Pointe, Suite # 6
Del Mar, California 92014
(858) 792-7463
http://www.edreferral.com

Gürze Books
P.O. Box 2238
Carlsbad, CA 92018
(800) 756-7533
http://www.bulimia.com

Harvard Eating Disorders
Center
356 Boylston Street
Boston, MA 02116
(617) 236-7766
http://www.hedc.org

Healing Connections
1461A First Avenue
Suite 303
New York, NY 10021
(212) 585-3450
http://www.healing
connections.org

International Association of
Eating Disorders
Professionals (IAEDP)
427 Whooping Loop, # 1819
Altamonte Springs, Florida
32701
(800) 800-8126
http://www.iaedp.com

National Association of
Anorexia Nervosa and
Associated Disorders
(ANAD)
P.O. Box 7
Highland Park, IL 60035
(847) 831-3438
http://www.anad.org

Chapter Notes

Chapter 1. The Enemy is Food

1. Mary Jo Malone, "A Battle Over a Life, So Fraught with Irony," *St. Petersburg Times*, May 3, 2001.

2. NOVA Online, "Dying to be Thin," December 6–20, 2000, <http://www.pbs.org/wgbh/nova/thin/story.html> (March 8, 2001).

3. Ibid.

4. American Psychiatric Association, *Diagnostic and Statistical Manual of Mental Disorders*, Fourth Edition (Washington, D.C.: American Psychiatric Association, 1994), p. 542.

5. Quoted in Michelle Tauber and Margaret Nelson, "The Thin Man: It's Not Just Women: Dr. Thomas Holbrook, A Recovering Anorexic, Helps Other Men Face Their Eating Disorders," *People Weekly*, September 25, 2000, pp. 13, 79.

6. Harvard Eating Disorders Center, "Facts and Findings," <http://www.hedc.org> (March 10, 2001); U.S. Department of Health and Human Services, Office on Women's Health, *Body Wise Handbook*, Second Edition, 2000; Anorexia Nervosa and Related Eating Disorders, "ANRED Statistics," <http://www.anred.com/stats.html> (March 10, 2001).

7. *Eating Disorders & Diabetes*, <http://www.eatingdisorder resources.com/diabetesforecast040197eds.html> (September 17, 2002).

8. "Behind the Scenes With the Famous and the Fascinating," *USA Today*, February 4, 1993.

9. learnFREE, "Eating Disorders," <http://www.mental-health-illness-info.com/eating-disorder/01d.htm> (October 7, 2001).

10. Quoted in American Anorexia Bulimia Association press release, "Magali Amedei Tells All about Her Battle with Bulimia; First Top Model to Publicly Admit Having an Eating Disorder," November 1999, <http://www.aabainc.org/outreach_tour/press_release.html> (October 12, 2001).

11. NOVA Online, "Ask the Experts," *Dying to be Thin*, December 15, 2000, <http://www.pbs.org/wgbh/nova/thin/ask_d_001215.html>, (September 16, 2002).

Chapter 2. The History of Anorexia and Bulimia

1. Joan Jacobs Brumberg, *Fasting Girls: The History of Anorexia Nervosa* (New York: Vintage Books/Random House, 2000), p. 46.

2. American Psychiatric Association, *Diagnostic and Statistical Manual of Mental Disorders*, Fourth Edition (Washington, D.C.: American Psychiatric Association, 1994), p. 583.

3. Anorexia Nervosa and Related Eating Disorders, Inc., "Frequently Asked Questions," 2002, <http://www.anred.com/faq.html> (September 16, 2002).

4. Brumberg, pp. 43–44.

5. William N. Davis in Rudolph M. Bell, *Holy Anorexia* (Chicago: University of Chicago Press, 1987), p. 181.

6. Jennifer Egan, "Power Suffering," *New York Times Magazine*, May 16, 1999, pp. 108–112.

7. Frances M. Berg, *Children and Teens Afraid to Eat: Helping Youth in Today's Weight-Obsessed World*, Third Edition (Hettinger, N. Dak.: Healthy Weight Network, 2001), p. 46.

8. Amy Dickinson, "Measuring Up: Obesity in Young Boys is on the Rise, and So Are Eating Disorders," *Time*, November 20, 2000, p. 154.

9. Remarks by the President at the U.S. Conference of Mayors, The White House, Office of the Press Secretary, press release, May 21, 1997.

10. Debra Waterhouse, *Like Mother, Like Daughter: How Women Are Influenced by Their Mothers' Relationship with Food—and How to Break the Pattern* (New York: Hyperion, 1997), p. 95.

11. Alison E. Field, Lilian Cheung, Anne M. Wolf, David B. Herzog, Steven L. Gortmaker, and Graham A. Colditz, "Exposure to the Mass Media and Weight Concerns among Girls," *Pediatrics*, March 3, 1999, p. E36.

12. Harvard Eating Disorders Center, "Facts and Findings," <http://www.hedc.org> (September 16, 2002).

13. Quoted in Elizabeth Mehren, "Negative Self-Image Starts Early," *Los Angeles Times*, March 5, 2001, pp. S1, S6.

14. Emily Wax, "Immigrant Girls Are Starving To Be American, Studies Find," *Washington Post*, electronic version, March 6, 2000.

Chapter 3. Detecting Anorexia

1. Quoted in "Thin in Hollywood," *Entertainment Tonight*, February 2, 2001.

2. Ibid.

3. Quoted in Paula Chin and Giovanna Breau, "Emotional Rescue," *People Weekly*, November 8, 1999, p. 18.

4. Quoted in "Going Public," *Maclean's*, January 18, 1999, p. 59.

5. Marilyn S. Massey-Stokes, "Prevention of Disordered Eating among Adolescents," *The Clearing House*, July 2000, pp. 6, 335.

6. National Association of Anorexia Nervosa and Associated Eating Disorders, "Facts about Eating Disorders," <http://www.anad.org/facts.htm> (September 16, 2002).

7. American Psychiatric Association, *Diagnostic and Statistical Manual of Mental Disorders*, Fourth Edition (Washington, D.C.: American Psychiatric Association, 1994), pp. 544–545.

8. Ibid.

9. Judy Tam Sargent, "Judy's Story—Frequently Asked Questions," <http://www.angelfire.com/ms/anorexianervosa/questions.html> (September 16, 2002).

10. Judy Tam Sargent and Sonia Nordenson (Contributor), *The Long Road Back, A Survivor's Guide to Anorexia* (Georgetown, Mass.: North Star Publications, 1999), p. ix.

11. Quoted in Michelle Tauber and Margaret Nelson, "The Thin Man: It's Not Just Women: Dr. Thomas Holbrook, A Recovering Anorexic, Helps Other Men Face Their Eating Disorders," *People Weekly*, September 25, 2000, pp. 13, 79.

12. NOVA Online, "Dying to be Thin," December 12, 2000 <http://www.pbs.org/wgbh/nova/thin/story.html> (September 16, 2002).

Chapter 4. Recognizing Bulimia

1. Personal interview with Karen Hamilton, January 21, 2001.

2. Quoted in author correspondence with Delta Dental Plan of Michigan, February 2001.

3. American Psychiatric Association, *Diagnostic and Statistical Manual of Mental Disorders*, Fourth Edition (Washington, DC: American Psychiatric Association, 1994), pp. 549–550.

4. Medlineplus Drug Information, "Ipecac (Oral)," <http:www.nlm.nih.gov/medlineplus/druginfo/uspdi/202605.html> (October 9, 2001).

5. Quoted in "A Conquering Heroine: High Noon's Maria Conchita Alonso Waged a Decade-long Battle with Bulimia," *People Weekly*, August 21, 2000, p. 69.

6. Ibid.

7. Quoted in Amrit Dhillon, "Fear of Being Fat; Why Young Women Are Prey to Eating Disorders," *Washington Post*, electronic version, April 13, 1999.

8. Well Connected, "Eating Disorders: Anorexia and Bulimia," *WebMD*, <http://www.my.webmd.com/index> March 1999.

9. Quoted in John Tischner, "Help for Eating Disorders," *The Suncoast News*, April 18, 2001, p. 1.

10. Beth M. McGilley and Tamara L. Pryor, "Assessment and Treatment of Bulimia Nervosa," *American Family Physician*, June 1998, p. 2743.

11. Brandie Greene as told to Leslie Leahy and correspondence with the author, March 2001.

Chapter 5. Binge Eating Disorder

1. Juli A. Goldfein, Michael J. Devlin, and Robert L. Spitzer, "Cognitive Behavioral Therapy for the Treatment of Binge Eating Disorder: What Constitutes Success?" *American Journal of Psychiatry*, July 2000, p. 1051.

2. American Psychiatric Association, *Diagnostic and Statistical Manual of Mental Disorders*, Fourth Edition (Washington, D.C.: American Psychiatric Association, 1994), pp. 550, 729.

3. Ibid., p. 550.

4. U.S. Department Of Health and Human Services, National Institutes of Health, "Binge Eating Disorders," brochure, February 2001; Michael D. Myers, M.D., "Obesity and Binge Eating Disorder," August 2001, <http://www.weight.com/Psychological/bed.html> (September 17, 2002).

5. Something Fishy Web site on Eating Disorders, "Compulsive (Over) Eating," <http://www.something=fishy.org> (September 17, 2002).

6. U.S. Department of Health and Human Services, National Institutes of Health, "Binge Eating Disorder," February 2001, <http://www.niddk.nih.gov/health/nutrit/pubs/binge.htm> (October 11, 2001).

7. Something Fishy Web site on Eating Disorders, "Personal Stories," <http://www.something-fishy.org/whatarethey/coe_stories1.php> (September 17, 2002).

8. Christopher G. Fairburn, Helen A. Doll, Sarah L. Welch, Phillipa J. Hay, Beverley A. Davies, Marianne E. O'Connor, "INSERT TITLE OF ESSAY OR ARTICLE," *Archives of General Psychiatry*, May 1998, pp. 425–432.

9. Frances M. Berg, *Children and Teens Afraid to Eat: Helping Youth in Today's Weight-Obsessed World*, Third Edition (Hettinger, N. Dak.: Healthy Weight Network, 2001), p. 142.

10. Office on Women's Health, Department of Health and Human Services, "Binge Eating Disorder FAQs," October 23, 2000, <http://www.4woman.gov/faq/bingeeating.htm> (September 17, 2002).

11. Berg, p.153.

Chapter 6. How Eating Disorders Are Treated

1. David M. Garner, et al. "Eating Attitudes Test (Eat-26)," (1982) <http://www.river=centre.org/ED_Index.html> (September 17, 2002).

2. HealthyPlace.com, "Eating Disorders Hospitalization and Treatment Online Conference," <http://www.healthyplace.com/Communities/Eating_Disorders/concernedcounseling/transcripts/eating_disorders_diagnosis_treatment.htm> (September 17, 2002).

3. Thomas L. Holbrook, M.D., "The Treatment of Eating Disorders," flyer (Oconomowoc, WI: Eating Disorder Center at Rogers Memorial Hospital, 2000), unpaged.

4. HealthyPlace.com, "Transcript from Online Conference on: Eating Disorders Hospitalization," <http://www.healthyplace.com/Communities/Eating_Disorders/concernedcounseling/transcripts/eating disorders_hospitalization.htm> (September 17, 2002).

5. NOVA Online, "Ask the Experts—Answers from Dr. Craig Johnson," December 19, 2000, <http://www.pbs.org/wgbh/nova/thin/ask_j_001219.html> (September 17, 2002).

Chapter 7. Treatment and Recovery Costs

1. Eileen Hoffman, M.D., *Our Health, Our Lives: A Revolutionary Approach to Total Health Care for Women* (New York: Pocket Books, 1995), p. 340.

2. Healing Connections, Inc., <http://www.healingconnections.org/hc3.htm> (September 17, 2002).

3. The National Association of Anorexia Nervosa and Associated Disorders, "Fight Insurance Discrimination," <http://www.anad.org/fight.htm> (September 17, 2002).

4. Author correspondence with Alicia Khoo, March, 2001.

5. Author correspondence with Ralph Kopald and Nissa Beth Gay, March 5, 2001.

Chapter 8. Awareness and Prevention Programs

1. Quoted in author correspondence with Kathryn Sylva, February, 2001.

2. "Tips for Becoming a Critical Viewer of the Media," <http://www.edap.org/media2.html> (March 10, 2001).

3. Media Awareness Network, "Kellogg's Special K advertisement," <http://www.media=awareness.ca/eng/med/class/teamedia/special3.htm> (September 17, 2002).

4. H.R. 46 introduced in the U.S. House of Representatives, January 3, 2001, <http://www.thomas.loc.gov> (September 17, 2002).

5. Quoted in Shana McNally, Associated Press, "'Go Girls' Tackles Teens' Heavy Issues of Weight, Image," *Seattle Times,* electronic version, March 19, 2000.

Chapter 9. Current and Future Research

1. Quoted in Daniel J. DeNoon, "Anti-Nausea Drug Helps Bulimics," *WebMD*, (September 17, 2002), <http://my.webmd.com/content/article/1728.55389> (March 10, 2001); Patricia L. Faris, Suck Won Kim, William H. Meller, Robert L. Goodale, Scott A. Oakman, Randall D. Hofbauer, Anne M. Marshall, Randall S. Daughters, Devjani Banerjee-Stevens, Elke D. Eckert, and Boyd K Hartman, "Effect Of Decreasing Afferent Vagal Activity With Ondansetron On Symptoms Of Bulimia Nervosa: A Randomised, Double-Blind Trial," Abstract, *The Lancet,* March 4, 2000, p. 792.

2. DeNoon.

3. "Blocking The Binge: UF Researchers Explore Treatment for Uncontrolled Eating," The Health Science Center, Office of Public Information, University of Florida, Press Release, August 9, 1999, <http://www.napa.ufl.edu/99news/binge.htm> (September 17, 2002).

4. Maria L. Chang, "Walking a Thin Line," *Science World,* December 14, 1998, p. 11.

Further Reading

Bode, Janet. *Food Fight*. New York: Simon & Schuster, 1997.

Gottlieb, Lori. *Stick Figure: A Diary of My Former Self*. New York: Simon & Schuster, 2000.

Graves, Bonnie B. *Anorexia*. Mankato, Minn.: Capstone Press, Inc., 2000.

Hall, Lindsey, and Leigh Cohn. *Bulimia: A Guide to Recovery*, Fifth Edition. Carlsbad, Calif.: Gürze Books, 1999.

Johnson, Marlys. *Understanding Exercise Addiction*. New York: Rosen Publishing Group, Ltd., 2000.

Maine, Margo, and Craig L. Johnson (photographer). *Father Hunger: Fathers, Daughters, and Food*. Carlsbad, Calif.: Gürze Books, 1991.

Normandi, Carol Emery and Lauralee Roark. *Over It: A Teen's Guide to Getting Beyond Obsession With Food and Weight*. New York: New World Library, 2001.

Sacker, Ira M., and Marc A. Zimmer. *Dying to Be Thin: Understanding and Defeating Anorexia and Bulimia*. New York: Warner Books, 1995.

Simpson, Carolyn. *A Teen Eating Disorder Prevention Book: Finding Answers*. New York: Rosen Publishing Group, Ltd., 2000.

Smith, Erica. *When Food Is the Enemy*. New York: Rosen Publishing Group, Ltd., 1998.

Internet Addresses

National Eating Disorders Association
http://www.nationaleatingdisorders.org

The Something Fishy Web Site on Eating Disorders
http://www.something-fishy.org

United States Department of Health and Human Services
Office on Women's Health
*The BodyWise Eating Disorders Information Packet for Middle
School Personnel*
http://www.4women.gov/BodyImage/Bodywise/bodywise.
htm

Index